Harry Thurston Peck

The Personal Equation

Harry Thurston Peck

The Personal Equation

ISBN/EAN: 9783742897510

Manufactured in Europe, USA, Canada, Australia, Japa

Cover: Foto ©Thomas Meinert / pixelio.de

Manufactured and distributed by brebook publishing software
(www.brebook.com)

Harry Thurston Peck

The Personal Equation

THE PERSONAL EQUATION

BY

HARRY THURSTON PECK

NEW YORK AND LONDON

HARPER & BROTHERS PUBLISHERS

1898

CONTENTS

WILLIAM DEAN HOWELLS

WILLIAM DEAN HOWELLS

MR. HOWELLS has essayed so many kinds of literary work, and has won so much deserved distinction in them all, as to make it very difficult to know from just what point of view one should regard him in considering his writings as a whole. It is, of course, primarily as a novelist that the popular mind will always think of him; yet when we come to analyze the meaning of his work, and seek to grasp the underlying motive of it all, it will be quite apparent to the analyst that fiction is but one particular expression of a spirit that pervades his other literary work as well; and that the novel is, at most, only one medium of several by which he has endeavored to effect a given purpose. A broad survey of all his writings will, I think, reveal that purpose in making clear the fact that it is really as a critic that we ought to view him, and in giving us the critic's motive as the fundamental basis for a final judgment of his place in literature.

It is not, however, merely as a literary critic that he most demands attention. One finds it quite impossible to narrow a consideration of his genius in such a way as this. Mr. Howells, to be sure, as well as others, is a critic of literature, and he is a very searching and suggestive critic, too; but one cannot even touch upon his literary criticism without feeling that in reality it is but a part, and a comparatively unimportant part, of his wider criticism of life; and that the same is true of every other phase of his intellectual activity when regarded separately and alone. This can, indeed, be said more broadly of Mr. Howells than of any other English-speaking author. Mr. Henry James, no doubt, is also in a way a critic of life; but his little corner of observation is so very little, his lenses are so carefully adjusted to one particular focus, and his instrument is so obviously an opera-glass and not a telescope, as to make his books the impressions of a first-nighter rather than the accurate and cosmic view of a sociological astronomer. Mr. Howells, on the other hand, has swept the whole horizon of his time; and it is not, therefore, merely as an essayist or as a novelist or as a poet that we must consider him, but as one who in his criticism and his fiction and his poetry alike has set before himself the task of picturing the life of his own age and of analyzing its spirit and its tendencies.

It is, of course, in fiction that his work has been most fully carried out ; and, therefore, chiefly from his fiction one obtains the truest insight into all his intellectual processes, and the best examples also of his critical felicities and his fundamental limitations. The circumstance that fiction is his chosen field of effort gives the subject a peculiar interest, because it involves a glance at the question of the American Novel—the question whether there has yet been written, or whether there is ever to be written, a kind of fiction that Americans shall recognize as essentially national, not only in its theme and color, but in its external form and literary technique.   .

Now, as to the American Novel when regarded from one point of view, one cannot help agreeing on the whole with Mr. Rollo Ogden's witty and, in the main, most sensible contentions. It is, indeed, absurd to suppose that, after all the centuries of creation and experiment which lie between Parthenius and Rudyard Kipling, we are going to witness the evolution of some new and striking literary manner, some principle of constructive art that no one has hitherto perceived, some tremendous *epochemachend* discovery that shall do for fiction what steam and electricity have done for mechanics, and that shall subtly harmonize with the material bigness and boisterousness of our native land. This vaguely fascinating dream has not, however, been altogether valueless. It has given the young brood of magazine-writers a theme of perennial interest, over which they can moult their literary pinfeathers at twenty dollars a page, and it has provided the American public with a pleasant if evanescent sensation perhaps once in every six months; for at intervals of just about this length the joyous announcement has gone forth that now at last *the* American Novel has been written; and then the literary tom-toms have been violently beaten, and every one in the Literary Shop has whooped it up so long as people could be induced to listen to the row, and until they have gone back again to the reading of English novels that are not constructed on a scientific theory or from patriotic motives, but are simply good, strong specimens of writing that grip the reader's attention, and make him willing and even eager to part with his money for more of the same sort.

Therefore, in this sense of the word, one need not be looking for an American novel as distinct from an English or a French or a Scandinavian or an Italian or a Græco-Roman novel. It may be assumed that the resources of fiction-writing are just as thoroughly well known as they ever will be; that all the appliances of the art have been discovered and tested long ago; that no amount of taking thought will add a single item to the technical equipment which is at the service of every novelist to-day; and that whenever a really great novel is produced, it is great because of the man behind the book, and not because of any fine-spun theory which the book itself exemplifies. A heaven-born artist does not spend the best years of his life in hunting up new colors for his palette. It is only a servant-maid who makes a poor pen an excuse for her bad spelling. And so in fiction-writing, if the *vivida vis* inflame the writer, it doesn't make the slightest difference whether he is an Idealist or a Romanticist or a Realist or a Naturalist or a Symbolist or a Sensitivist or a happy combination of all six. If he have it in him to write an immortal novel he will write it, and that is all there is to it.

Nevertheless, from another point of view,

one may truly speak of the American Novel as a thing apart, because of the great difficulty in the conditions that attend its successful composition. The American Novel, as we understand it, is not to be a novel constructed on hitherto unheard-of lines, or by some new formula thoughtfully evolved by American writers; but a novel that shall give an adequate and accurate delineation of the life that is lived only in this huge, loose-hung, colossus of a country—a kind of life to which the history of the world affords no parallel whatever. When the Englishman or when the Frenchman sits down to write a novel, he has no difficulty in getting his social *mise en scène* to suit him; he need not, indeed, give it any particular thought at all. The social system that he knows is one whose framework is definite, well ordered, compact, and perfectly intelligible even to the casual foreigner. Everything has its place; everything is regulated and understood; everything, in fact, is obvious and explicable. His background is, in a way, already filled in, and it is only figure-painting that he has to do.

But how strangely different is the case with one who seeks to fix upon his canvas a true impression of American life! A vast kaleido-

scopic mass of color lies before him, shifting
and changing with every touch, a society in a
fluid state, heterogeneous, anomalous, bizarre,
and shot all through with a million piquant
incongruities. The boundless wealth and the
squalid poverty, the splendor and the crudity,
the magnificence and the cheapness, the reck-
lessness and the conservatism, the cynicism
and the faith, the intellectual keenness and
the unspeakable fatuity, the strong common-
sense and the foolish gullibility, the defiant
arrogance and the patient meekness, the commercial acuteness and the political stupidity—
can any one bring out all these wonderful contrasts in the national character, and yet preserve the slightest trace of verisimilitude and
probability? And the strange medley of humanity—the washer-woman of the diggings
blossoming out into the *grande dame* who entertains kings and gives her daughters in marriage to princes, the young girl with her
" chaste depravity," the emancipated woman,
the canal-boy fighting his way to the headship
of the nation, the keen-eyed business man who
is to-day cornering the market and to-morrow
haranguing the Senate and the day after bringing out an edition of a classic, the curious bits
of foreign life and custom embedded in the

midst of an Anglo-Saxon people, and under-
neath it all a great compact mass of strong
and simple and conservative men and women,
bearing up the rest and giving cohesion and
stability to the whole structure. Any one can
tell of all these things ; any one can sketch
them separately and in detail ; but who is able
and who will ever be able to give one luminous
picture of them as a single entity, each in its
true relation to the rest, with a sense of proportion and relativity, and in such a way as to
make one see and feel the truth of it all?

No such problem ever before confronted the
novelist ; yet it is not until this problem has
been solved that the American Novel in its
largest sense will have an actual existence. To
begin with, there is not even such a thing as
an American type. There is a New England
type, and there is a Southern type, and there
is a Far Western type ; but even these are
not perfectly defined, but shade off into each
other with many an imperceptible *nuance*, while
between them lie all sorts of individual and
quite distinctive groups which an American
easily recognizes, even though he cannot so
easily describe them. In no country in the
world are there so many local points of difference ; for not only are a Bostonian and a New-

Yorker and a Philadelphian and a Chicagoan
and a San Franciscan essentially unlike, but
there are distinctions quite as clearly though
more subtly to be drawn between a Buffalonian and a Syracusan, between a Baltimorean
and a Charlestonian, between a Peorian and a
Topekan. These people do not even speak
an absolutely identical language, but display
such dialectic variations as make the difference of habitat immediately perceptible to the
ear of a native. It is only the self-satisfied
Englishman who ignores all these bewildering
complications. He, of course, with the smug
complacency of his kind, will talk with half a
dozen Americans, read a few American newspapers, and then introduce into his next novel
a "Yankee heiress" or a "Senator from Mi-
kewa" with characteristics evolved from the
writer's inner consciousness, and speaking a
dialect the like of which was never heard from
the mouth of any human being, but which is
far more grotesque than if an American novelist should represent an Englishman speaking a blend of Cockney jargon, Dublin Irish,
Yorkshire dialect, Welsh *patois*, and Lowland
Scotch.

Yet though foreigners do not understand
the complicated difficulties that beset the

one who tries to limn in a large way the life
and attributes of the American people, our
own writers are fully aware of them ; and
hence it is that they have given us, in the
main, not the American Novel, but novels
written in America, which is a very different
thing. It is not likely that any better work
will be done than much of that which already
reveals some of the strange nooks and corners
of American life. No one, for example, could
show a subtler knowledge of New England
than Miss Wilkins brings to her intensely
vital delineations; no one will ever make us
feel more intensely the spirit of the North-
west than Mr. Hamlin Garland does; no one
will better draw the dull, raw life of the little
towns of Central and Western New York than
Mr. Harold Frederic; no one will have a fuller
understanding of certain phases of existence in
the American metropolis than has Mr. Brander
Matthews. But who is to come forth equipped with the knowledge and the insight and
the vivid power necessary to draw the picture
as a whole, and with a master's touch to fling
before us the great national cosmos in its en-
tirety—vital, convincing, real?

But, says some one, there is Mr. Howells;
and sure enough, if we grant that Mr. Howells

has not succeeded in this task, then so far no
one has succeeded. Indeed, we might say *a
priori* that Mr. Howells is the one living
writer who by the circumstances of training,
experience, and exceptional gifts ought to
grapple successfully with the difficulties that
have proved insurmountable to so many others.
Born in one of the Central Western States at
a time when these were still in the making,
his most impressionable years were spent amid
influences that gave him at first hand an intimate knowledge of American life in its evo-
lutionary stage. In an intensely American
community, among those who typified all the
primitive American virtues of courage, indus-
try, integrity, and thrift, he looked upon the
nation-builders as they did their work, and
drank in the subtlest understanding of that
stratum of society which is the base of the
whole gigantic system. And for his purpose
it was lucky that he never had the academic
training, which, though it sharpens the critical
powers, too often narrows the sympathies and
deadens the creative faculty. He lived his
early years as one of the people, as a printer,
as a newspaper reporter, recording continually
his impressions, learning the art of writing in
a school that teaches clearness, vividness, and

compression, and being all the time in touch
with the multifarious types that daily flit before the keen eye of the American journalist.
In 1860, with his appointment by President
Lincoln as Consul to Venice, began the other
side of his preliminary training. From the
raw and unformed civilization of the West he
passed at once to an environment that was
absolutely antithetical, to an atmosphere permeated with memories of old-time magnificence and eloquent of art—an atmosphere instinct with sensuous beauty, in which all sorts
of exquisite half-tints become perceptible, and
in which the mind awakens to subtle meanings and delicate discriminations. This curious
change from Columbus to the Canalazzo, from
the Muskingum to Malamocco, was of all
things the most ideal as a phase in the training of the literary artist. It gave to him a
wholly different point of view, a new standard
of comparison, a sense of values and of proportion, and enabled him to see more clearly
and with a truer perspective the other life that
he had left behind him. Returning to the
United States, his experience was enlarged in
still different surroundings when he took the
editorship of the *Atlantic Monthly* and for
many years made one of the set which in those

days stood for all that was refined and cultivated in American letters. The circle of his
experience was completed when he passed
from Boston to New York and made his home
in the cosmopolitan whirl of the American
metropolis.

An experience and a training such as these,
the like of which are rare indeed, could scarcely fail to give to their possessor a marvellous
power, if coupled with the requisite natural
gifts. And Mr. Howells has these gifts. A
quick eye for what is striking in individuals
or in life, a wonderful photographic instinct for
detail, a shrewd insight into human motive, a
truly American perception of the ludicrous, a
natural gift of language, a talent for crystalliz-
ing in a phrase or an epithet the essential attribute of any subject, a Frenchman's reverence for *le mot juste*—all these superimposed
upon an experience so broad as to be national
rather than sectional, and with the advantage
of an international point of view, may surely
warrant one in saying what has just been said :
that if Mr. Howells has not written the American Novel, then no one else as yet has written
it. And, indeed, whether he has written it or
not, he has at any rate received a reward com-
mensurate with his native gifts and his excep-

tional endowment. He is to-day the most eminent of all living American men of letters.
As a novelist he is one of the greatest that our
country has yet produced. A new book from
his pen is always regarded as an important
literary event. His name is known and hon-
ored wherever the English language is understood. But has he, as a matter of fact, succeeded at any time in writing the American
Novel and not merely clever novels of American life written in America by an American?

It may, perhaps, at first sight seem fanciful,
but there can really be little doubt that the
limitations which have prevented Mr. Howells
from attaining supreme success as a fiction-
writer, and that have made his general theory
of criticism and of life inadequate, are to be
traced directly to certain circumstances which
have already been narrated. The first is his
long residence in Boston, and the second is
his subsequent identification with New York.
Naturally, a thesis such as this requires some
specific elucidation and defence.

One of these days a work will, perhaps, be
written upon the topograpical aspects of literature, and in it at least one long chapter will
have to be devoted to the influence of Boston
upon American letters. Everybody knows

what Boston is—one of the most interesting,
and perhaps the most absolutely individual, of
American cities. It has a distinctive character
and a distinctive flavor that no one has ever
failed to recognize. The character is decidedly pronounced, and the flavor is a little tart,
with something of what the Boston dialect
would describe as a "tang"; but both are
wholesome, and, in a way, agreeable. Boston
shows us, in fact, almost the sole survival upon
American soil of a purely English influence—
an influence seen alike in the city's external
appearance, in the temperament of its people,
and in their intellectual characteristics. Yet
this strong suggestion of England never recalls
semi-cosmopolitan London with its multitudi-
nous interests and its consciousness of contact
with the whole wide world. It is rather a suggestion of Leicester mingled with Leeds and
perhaps a dash of Edinburgh—in fact, of a
community not directly in touch with anything
beyond its own borders, but very self-centred
and compact, and taken up wholly with its
own concerns. Its colonialism stands out all
over it with both the virtues and the defects
of its quality. There are all the integrity
of purpose, all the anxious uneasiness about
"duty," the intense self-respect and self-reli-

2

ance of the New-Englander, the love of truth
and justice, the independence and the recti-
tude ; but there can be found also all the intolerance, all the narrowness, all the impenetrable complacency, and all the intellectual
myopia of the provincial Englishman.

Charles Reade, in one of his novels, gives a
series of maps to illustrate the point of view
of the average English squire.   His own county is first depicted in a large, clear map, with
its smallest localities carefully noted ; a second
map shows England as a whole, about half as
large ; then in a third map, drawn very small,
is displayed the rest of the world covering a
space of about the size of one's thumb-nail.
Now this is precisely the way in which a true
Bostonian would set forth respectively the
town of Boston, the United States as a whole,
and the rest of the world, if he were to express his real feelings in terms of comparative
cartography ; and it simply means that Boston's true affinities are not at all with the great
cities of the earth, but with the provincial English towns.   It has their atmosphere to perfection ; so that although we know, as a matter
of fact, that its customs are in reality those of
the civilized world at large, one never meets a
Boston man without a certain vague, yet irre-

pressible feeling that he probably dines at five
o'clock in the afternoon, and has a sweet champagne served with the fish.

The truest expression of the Boston spirit
in literature is undyingly preserved in the work
of Oliver Wendell Holmes, whose claim to immortality is to be found above all in this, that
he is the quintessence of Boston, which is in
itself the quintessence of New England ; and
both his foreign travel and his belief in his
own cosmopolitanism only serve to give a more
striking background to his intense provincialism, and to enhance its piquant flavor.   In his
verse we find much less to make us think of
Hippocrene than of the "kag" of cider.   The
poetic draught substitutes for the sparkle of
the vintage of Champagne the nip of the gin-
ger that gives life to the home-brewed switchel.
It is not the poet of tradition who in Holmes
appears to be singing to us, but more often
the village bard, whose verses appear with
beautiful regularity in the left-hand upper corner of the county newspaper, and who has his
neat little copy of rhymes for every celebration, from the dinner of the village fire-com-
pany to the opening of the ladies' oyster-sup-
per for the benefit of the Orthodox Church.
In like manner, when we read certain passages

of the *Autocrat*, we can shut our eyes and pass
behind the ostensible personality of the author to his real prototype—the country smarty
whose reputation as a funny fellow draws a
group of admiring rustics about him as he sits
on a cracker-barrel in the village "store" and
emits his jokes, pausing only to refresh himself from a contiguous cheese, and to spit pro-
fusely upon the cast-iron stove. It may be
frankly conceded that the wit is genuine,
though suggesting Italian vinegar rather than
Attic salt; but it is intensely local, and its
similes and metaphors all smack of the cider-
mill, the quilting-bee, the town-meeting, and
the "vendue."

The influence of long contact with a community whose spirit is such as this must necessarily stimulate self-consciousness and an in-
trospection that may easily become morbid in
its intensity. Yet its effects might well be salu-
tary to one whose own temperament lacked re-
pression and subjectivity. Unfortunately, Mr.
Howells already possessed these qualities in
excess. Just as the late Edward Henry Palmer,
though born of English parents and in an English home, was, from the moment of his birth,
in every essential respect an Arab, so Mr.
Howells, though a native of Ohio, and sprung

from Welsh stock, has always been essentially
a New-Englander. The remarkable self-analysis of his early mentality which he has given
us in *A Boy's Town* proves this beyond a doubt.
It shows him even as a child to have been
self-conscious, introspective, abnormally prone
to dwell upon his own sensations and emotions, and to exaggerate them out of all proportion to their real importance. This is the
true New England temperament, rooted in individualism, pushing self-analysis to the point
of torture, regarding details as of infinite significance, teaching that the part is greater than
the whole, and robbing its possessor of a sense
of true proportion. But to the literary artist,
as to the philosopher, the sense of proportion
is everything; for it is the one sovereign anti-
dote to provincialism, philistinism, and morbidity. It and a sense of humor are God's
greatest gifts to man; and the first of these
He seems in His infinite wisdom to have de-
nied to the typical New-Englander, who, in
politics and religion and literature alike, out-
does Protagoras in devotion to the doctrine
that the individual is the measure of all things.

That Mr. Howells, with New England traits
already so sharply accentuated, should have
been definitely and irrevocably stamped with

the New England influence, must therefore be
regarded as a distinct misfortune to American
literature; for it has narrowed his marvellous
gifts of delineation to a single sphere and made
him the novelist of a section, when his genius
might otherwise have become broadly national. This consideration fully answers the question whether he has written the American
Novel, for it shows that he has not; that fate
had determined that he should merely write
the Novel of New England. This, indeed, he
has actually done. He has given us a single
novel that is really great, another that is nearly great, and one absolutely perfect story; and
each of these is New England to the core.

In *A Modern Instance* one sees what he
might have achieved but for the overmaster-
ing influence that has fettered and restricted
his gifts of portraiture. This book differs essentially from the general run of American
novels in its breadth and grasp and color, and
especially in being free from a certain thinness
that characterizes pretty nearly all the fiction
produced in the United States. American
novels almost invariably lack body and substance. They have a high, dry, rarefied atmosphere which may be very clear, but in which
it is very difficult to breathe for any length

of time. They may possess more subtlety than one finds in an English novel, but they are afflicted with so advanced an anæmia that one always turns from them with a sense of relief to the strong, well-nourished work of the Englishman who shows us bone and muscle and flesh and blood in place of mere nerves, with plenty of good port - wine and roast beef instead of angel-food and ether. But *A Modern Instance* has body to it, and color and movement and vitality. Nearly all of its characters are living, human beings, and not mere psychological studies. It is for this reason that one can read and re-read the book, and find several of its personages dwelling forever after in his memory, as do the men and women whom we have known in life. Bartley Hubbard, for example, is as real as Mr. Howells himself; and the proof of it is found in the fact that, in spite of his baseness and cheapness, we cannot refrain from feeling sorry for him and even at times from almost liking him, just as we feel sorry for him and almost like him when we meet him in our daily life. And Marcia and Kinney and Witherby and the old Squire are living beings, too. Mr. Howells has drawn them with more freedom and boldness than he often shows, and has given himself far less

concern about accumulating mere details.   He
has, moreover, in a measure cut loose from his
own pet theory of fiction-writing.   He has not
scrupled to give us some fine dramatic touches
after the manner of the Romanticists, and has
even led us up to an intensely powerful climax
in the scene where the quaintly pathetic figure
of Squire Gaylord rises in the Western court-
room and pleads for justice and for vengeance
in the last words that he ever utters.   And
this is one of the things that make for genuine
realism, because such striking scenes as these
are not so rare in life as Mr. Howells sometimes appears to think.   Altogether, one cannot say too much of *A Modern Instance*.   It
bears the true stamp of genius, and it will live
as long as anything that American literature
can show; for in it the writer stands aside and
lets the action evolve itself before the reader's
eye, and thus comes very near to meriting the
tribute which Hawthorne gave to the cyclo-
pean art of Anthony Trollope when he said
that in reading him it seems as though some
giant had hewn out a great lump of English
soil and set it down before us, with all the human beings on it going about their affairs unconscious of our observation.   And this is just
what Mr. Howells has done in *A Modern In-*

stance, only it is out of the soil of New England that he has hewn the lump.

The Rise of Silas Lapham is, as a whole, below the level of *A Modern Instance*, but it is still a masterly and memorable book. The character of Silas Lapham himself is by all odds the most remarkable piece of portraiture that Mr. Howells has ever done, and it is the only one that attains to the proportions of a broadly national type. The self-made man who works his way up the ladder of material prosperity was never more convincingly depicted; and the portrait is one that is true of the native American everywhere, East as well as West. Rooted in the soil of the farm, this homely figure with its heaviness and gentleness, its simplicity and shrewdness, its rugged honesty and worldly wisdom, its uncouthness and native humor, its quaint conceit and innocent pride tempered always with a hesitating self-depreciation, its eye to the main chance, and its haunting and remorseless conscientiousness —we see them all in this amusing yet profoundly touching creation, which is as vital as anything that human art has ever limned. The opening chapter where Lapham is interviewed by Bartley Hubbard for the *Events*, in the office of the "mineral-paint" manufactory, is a miracle of condensed pictorial power, in which each word goes with swiftness and precision to the mark. When we have finished it, we know the Colonel through and through in every stage of his career, and if the book had ended there, it would still have given to our native fiction a new and permanent possession.

In *The Lady of the Aroostook* we have the most perfect story that American literature has yet produced. It is the height of literary art, for its finish is as exquisite as its design. One can re-read it a score of times, and always with a fresh enjoyment of its unerring insight and convincing truth, and of the delicate humor that plays along its lines and heightens here and there the scenes of really unstudied emotion that are elsewhere so infrequent in our author's work. But the book is more than a perfect story ; it is a concrete illustration of a phase of American civilization, and one that could not be half so well explained in any other way. It depicts social conditions that to a foreigner are quite inexplicable, yet which an American understands so thoroughly that if he had not learned to know the foreign point of view, as Mr. Howells came to know it, it never would occur to him to set it forth in the form

of a story. Mr. Charles Dudley Warner has
made a very admirable use of some of the English criticism upon this book in showing how
certain of the conditions of American life differ *toto cœlo* from anything that a European
can understand. That Lydia Blood, a girl
from rural New England, and reared amid surroundings that are homely in the extreme,
should have all the delicacy and dignity of a
" lady," and that she should be considered by
the writer and by the personages of the story
to be a " lady," was as strange and improbable
to the foreign critic as that on reaching Venice
she should at once have taken with entire composure a lady's place in its society.

One dwells with fondness on this charming
story, which compresses within a hundred pages
so much rare portraiture, so much sympathetic knowledge, and so many delicate literary
graces. With the possible exception of Staniford, every single character in the book is
drawn to perfection, from Ezra Perkins, who
drives the Concord stage at South Bradfield,
and Aunt Maria and Captain Jenness, to the
curiously cosmopolitan circle of Mrs. Erwin's
set at Venice—Miss Landini, who invokes im-
partially the devil and the Deity in her conversation, Rose - Black, the crawling English

artist, Henshaw Erwin with his passion for collecting Americanisms, and Lydia herself, a second Marcia Hubbard, but with finer traits. Every one of these is sketched in with a firm hand and the most artistic sense of contrast ; and the changes of scene from South Bradfield to the ship, and from the ship to Venice, give a fascinating and varied background for the movement of the story. The last three or four pages would alone be sufficient to make a lasting reputation for their author, so perfect is the finish of the picture where Staniford, after marrying Lydia, goes with her to visit her old home at South Bradfield in the midst of winter. Mr. Howells has caught the exact feeling of the scene, the people, and the atmosphere, and each successive stroke so artfully heightens the effect that in reading one almost cries out with wonder and delight. The prim house walled in by snow-banks, the social evening with the minister and his wife, which Aunt Maria, after passing coffee and sponge-cake, felt to be so brilliant as to be almost wicked, and, above all, the symbolistic parlor-lamp of pea-green glass with a large red woollen wick — that parlor-lamp alone is a sufficient claim to immortality, for its glow, somehow or other, makes the whole life and

aspect of South Bradfield perceptible at a
glance.

The remembrance of this story heightens
one's regret that among all the other work that
Mr. Howells has given us, nothing else is found
quite worthy of being set beside it ; for as time
went on the spell of Boston grew stronger and
stronger upon him, and we find less and less of
the comparative freedom and spaciousness that
appear in the three fine books that we have
just enumerated. Individualism marked him
for its own. He began to abuse his gift of
observation. Instead of going always swiftly
and unerringly to the very heart of things, he
sometimes seemed to consider it sufficient to
accumulate a multiplicity of trivial details and
to let a microscopic fidelity take the place of
a broader sympathy. The keenness of vision
involved in some of his details is almost startling, but in the end this sort of thing defeats
its own purpose, for the reader is so astonished
by the photographic accuracy of the observer,
that his attention is distracted from the march
of events, and he can think only of how very
clever Mr. Howells is. In other words, the brilliancy of the novelist casts into a semi-shadow
the evolution of the novel, and Mr. Howells is
the fatally successful rival of his own creations.

It is precisely in this respect that Thackeray
too often suffers in comparison with Dickens ;
for although his art is infinitely greater, it is
not always the art that conceals itself, but an
art that is too consciously exposed to the reader's view.   Thus when Dickens takes us with
Pecksniff into Mrs. Todgers's immortal lodging-
house, we actually go there.   We snuff the
sickly gushes of soup with our own noses, we
see with our own eyes the worn-out floor-cloth
and the table with its splashes of gravy, we
hear with our own ears the convivial wit of
Mr. Jinkins and the other commercial gentlemen, and for the moment Dickens has nothing
to do with it at all.   But when Thackeray describes the similar *ménage* of the Gann family
in *A Shabby Genteel Story*, it is not we who
see it for ourselves, but it is Thackeray who is
telling us what he has seen.   We are kept in
a constant state of admiration over the extraordinary accuracy of his vision.   He is always present in his own person ; and, just as
Mr. George Brandon reported it all to the Vis-
count Cinqbars, so Thackeray reports it to us
and in a somewhat similar spirit, with a constant appeal to " the principle in us that sniffs."
It is all very brilliant ; but Mr. Howells has
himself admitted that it has its defects ; that

it is too sophisticated; and that if, by comparison, the magic of Dickens be rough magic and
wholly elemental, it is at least grandly elemental and deals with larger moods than those
that respond merely to tastes and preferences.

So it is that all of Mr. Howells's novels, except the ones already noted as exceptions, are
permeated with this suggestion of his own individuality, and with that excessive elaboration which prevents us from seeing the wood
by reason of the trees. The writer stands between us and his books. Moreover, though the
details of his work may be often remarkably
characteristic and typical, their combination
is not necessarily either characteristic or typical; and while his personages may be indi-
vidually realistic, in combination they are often quite unreal in that they show no life and
movement and spontaneity. One is reminded
by them of a painting in which every figure
is admirably finished, but in which, nevertheless, the effect of the whole is stiff and wood-
en. Mr. Howells's gallery, in other words,
contains an immense array of careful sketches,
but only a very few successful pictures. And
this is why of his later books even the most
conscientious reader retains only a shadowy
and confused impression. The titles and scenes

and plots (so far as there are any plots discernible) are all blurred and jumbled together ; and just a few strongly drawn individual portraits stand out in a hopeless if splendid isolation. One recalls the striking figure of the embezzler Northwick in *The Quality of Mercy*, wherein one scene is matchless in its psychology ; the gawky youth in *The Minister's Charge ;* Helen Harkness, the intensely Bostonian type of girl in *A Woman's Reason*, who thinks that "the Indian trade" confers an aristocratic *cachet ;* and possibly Clara Kingsbury, though one may express a conscientious doubt whether even in Boston the ladies of the Brahminical set are wont to speak of their "gentleman friends;" but what befell these persons the present writer, at least, is unable to recall ; and he has found it necessary, at the present time, in every case to search through his collection of Mr. Howells's books in order to be quite certain that he has assigned each character mentioned to its proper source.

The individual note is heard with even greater clearness in our author's literary criticism, for here it has appeared to him unnecessary to do much more than state his own opinions with a dogmatism which is not less real because it is so often mingled with felicitous phrases

and spiced with bits of epigram. Within the
last two or three years, in fact, he has begun
to issue books whose very titles—*My Literary
Passions* and *Impressions and Experiences*—
quite frankly indicate how purely personal to
himself his judgments are. In these books we
are told not only what opinions he has formed,
but the exact circumstances under which he
came to form them ; who first led him to read
this and that ; whether he was at home or at
his uncle's when he made his first acquaintance
with an author ; that he was shelling peas
when he first heard of *Don Quixote ;* that it
was his elder brother who introduced him to
Captain Marryat ; with an infinite deal of similar personal detail continuously presupposing
that the reader must regard these incidental
facts as of extreme importance. In his latest
volume he even devotes some thirty or forty
pages to the chronicle of his personal experiences with beggars.

In another writer this would be egoism of a
gigantic growth ; but in Mr. Howells it is only
the individualism of the New-Englander expressing itself in terms of literary criticism.
Yet to this sort of thing is due a good deal of
the exasperation that some of Mr. Howells's
opinions have excited ; for while they are sim-

ply the personal views of an individual, they
are sometimes put forth as though they were
meant to found a school of criticism and to
abolish the canons that have been built upon
the intellectual experience of centuries.   It
is all very well for Mr. Howells, as an individual, to thrust Romanticism into his ash-barrel,
as being nothing but a piece of literary junk;
but when he sets up as a master of criticism,
the matter comes to be of more importance,
and one may then quite reasonably question
alike his authority and his critical capacity.
A critic who prefers Realism to Romanticism
is well within his rights; but when he would
hoot Romanticism out of existence altogether
simply because it does not happen to appeal
to him, then we may properly suspect him of
a defective equipment.   The curious thing
about Mr. Howells is that he makes his own
inability to appreciate certain phases of literature an additional claim upon our attention.
Thus, in the chronicle of his literary passions,
he heads a chapter with the name of Scott,
apparently for the sole purpose of telling us,
as he does, that though he has read Scott's
novels, he did so wholly from a sense of duty,
and that little or nothing of them remains with
him at the present time.   Now when a literary

critic comes forward and declares that he has
found nothing touching and tender in the character of Jeanie Deans, nothing humorous in the
portrayal of Andrew Fairservice, nothing impressively terrible in the story of Ravenswood,
nothing breathlessly exciting in the unravel-
ling of Bertram's weird, and nothing that stirs
the blood like a trumpet-call in the splendid
pictures of chivalry that stud the pages of
Ivanhoe, and yet in the same breath announces
that Mr. J. W. De Forest is one of the greatest
of living novelists, then we may rightly liken
such a critic to a person who assures us of his
own ability as a judge of painting, and cites
as one of his chief qualifications the fact that
he is color - blind, and cannot tell blue from
green.

It is obvious that one so sensitive as Mr.
Howells to external impressions must be sensibly affected by his environment ; and here,
I think, is found an explanation of the comparative inferiority of many of his later novels.
This brings us to the second part of our original thesis—the effect upon his genius and its
expression of his final removal from Boston to
New York. One might argue, adducing the
facts already set forth, that this change was
precisely the thing needed to counteract the

excessive individuality and concentration of
his literary methods. But this line of argument leaves out of sight, first, the fact that
the change was made only after Mr. Howells's formative period was over, and that
hence it occurred too late; and it ignores,
in the second place, the peculiar influence
which New York exerts upon the typical Bostonian.

It was long ago remarked by some superficial observer that New York is in reality not
an American city at all; and the saying has
been so constantly repeated by those who
ought to have known better, that it has come
to be regarded as axiomatic in its truth. But
as a matter of fact, nothing could be more
absolutely false; for, apart from some of its
external characteristics, New York is the most
truly American city in existence—the only
city that has assimilated and moulded into a
whole all the attributes of our people, blend-
ing them so perfectly as to yield for a result
not a Northern or a Southern or an Eastern or
a Western product, but one that is simply and
typically American. And in doing this it has
happily eliminated one quality that is elsewhere the bane of the American temperament
—the quality of self-consciousness. For in its

own way the self-consciousness of Chicago,
for example, is as marked as the self-consciousness of Boston, only the manifestation of it
is different. Boston, being the old maid of
American cities, displays the self-consciousness
of primness; while Chicago, the hobbledehoy
of American cities, is troubled by the self-consciousness of overgrowth, and, so to speak, is
always concerned as to what to do with its
feet and hands, and troubled by the uneasy
consciousness that its legs are far too long;
while if it wishes to speak impressively, its
voice flies off the handle and ends in a falsetto
squeak. In either city the individual is the
unit of the whole, and is always sure of his own
importance. But New York, whose quality is
greatness rather than mere bigness, takes no
account of the individual, and the individual
knows it. The giant forces that are here at
play are too vast for any one to control. They
act and react with such a mighty sweep and
power as to dwarf the individual altogether,
who resembles a tiny bird that has built its
nest in the beam of some colossal engine. It
knows the movements of the great machine,
it does not dread it, and it even comes to love
it for its tremendous energy; but it would no
more think of trying to direct or check it than

one of us would think of bridling a cyclone or
staying the plunge of a water-spout.   In the
sphere of civics the immensity of this great
Weltstadt has its disadvantages, but from
every other point of view it is wonderful and
inspiring.   No single influence can affect it.
No great university can ever leaven it as Harvard has leavened Boston ; no great literary
movement can ever make an impression on
it ; no wave of religious excitement can ever
spread through all its channels ; no political
cataclysm can disorganize the play of its colossal forces.   Men of commanding influence
and national reputation come to New York,
and take their places meekly far down the line ;
an invading army would be run in by the po-
lice.   The giant swallows everything, takes everything to itself, and then moves on unconscious of it and unchanged.   Nothing can be
more inspiring to one who knows it well, and
who exults in the largeness and power and
magnificence of it all.

But the effect of it upon the Bostonian born
is very curious. Catch a typical Bostonian
and suddenly transfer him to the heart of
Brooklyn, or Philadelphia, or New Orleans, or
San Francisco, or even of Chicago, and while
he will recognize the unfamiliarity of his new

environment, it will not interfere with his enjoyment.   He is still an important individual;
he is still some one to be reckoned with; and
those who meet him will appreciate the fact
because they, too, are important individuals
who count.   But plump him down in the middle of New York, and the difference is startling.   A great bewilderment comes over him.
He feels that he has somehow got out of his
own snug little corner into a great whirl that
bewilders him and makes him dizzy.   He is
uneasily conscious that he has been dwarfed
to a mere human atom; his complacency vanishes; he knows that his importance has shrunk
into nothingness, and he doesn't like it.   He
resembles a small mouse that has crept timidly
out into a vast hall, and then, appalled by the
unwonted vista, scuds back to its hole with
squeaks of genuine dismay.

Mr. Howells has himself expressed this feeling in *Their Wedding Journey*, when Basil
March and Isabel, fresh from the city of the
triple mountain, stand before Grace Church
and gaze up and down Broadway.   And he
has, in spite of himself, distilled the same feeling into those books of his that, written under
the oppression of his new environment, convey
something of that oppression to his readers'

minds. In *A Hazard of New Fortunes* and *The World of Chance* one finds no more the unforced humor and the cheerful spontaneity of his earlier novels. He has become melancholy, and with the true New England sense of duty, he has begun to feel that he has a "mission."

It was in New York, apparently, that Mr. Howells made the discovery that while there are in the world people who have plenty of money, there are also people who haven't any at all to speak of ; that there are people who are harshly used by their employers, people who are often ill, people who live in squalid tenements—people, in a word, who are unhappy through no fault of their own. To a philosophical observer these and other facts of the kind discovered by Mr. Howells are hardly so pathetic as the thoroughly *naïf* surprise with which Mr. Howells suddenly became conscious of their existence ; and fully as pathetic also is the generous but quite inartistic impulse that has led him to spoil his novels in order to impart to others some knowledge of his discovery. For as soon as he began to write stories with an obvious *Tendenz* and permeated with all the uneasiness of the Bostonian who is consciously out of his element, the lit-

erary quality of his work deteriorated in a perceptible manner. Who can recall anything of
the two books just named except squalor, and
unhappiness, and cheap eating-houses, and
commonplace characters of all grades of fatuity, and a general feeling that the author evidently thinks the times are out of joint? And
so, doubtless, they are, and always were, for
that matter; but Mr. Howells is not going to
set them right by publishing vague pictures
of Altruria, and asperging all of us with his
diluted slops of Socialism. For everything
will go on precisely as before; and all that he
will have accomplished will be the transformation of a great literary artist into a gloomy and
ineffectual Bellamy.

But the depression which has grown upon
Mr. Howells in the past few years has extended beyond his view of existing social conditions, and has been formulated into a semi-
pessimistic theory of life. This phase of his
thought finds its fullest expression in his
verse, some of which is really remarkable in
its condensed expression of a sort of won-
dering despair, poignant and terrible. No
single poem better reveals this state of mind
than the following from his *Stops of Various
Quills:*

" I was not asked if I should like to come,
   I have not seen my host here since I came,
   Or had a word of welcome in his name.
 Some say that we shall never see him, and some
 That we shall see him elsewhere, and then know
   Why we were bid. How long I am to stay
   I have not the least notion. None, they say,
 Was ever told when he should come or go,
 But every now and then there bursts upon
   The song and mirth a lamentable noise,
   A sound of shrieks and sobs, that strikes our joys
 Dumb in our breasts ; and then, some one is gone.
   They say we meet him. None knows where or
      when.
   We know we shall not meet him here again."

And there comes up continually his old lament
over the inequality that everywhere marks the
lot of man. The sight of poverty makes him
shudder, and the sight of riches makes him
shudder, too. He draws us a picture of a gay
company dancing among scarlet flowers to the
sound of music, and then he goes on :

" I looked again and saw that flowery space
   Stirring as if alive, beneath the tread
   That rested now upon an old man's head
 And now upon a baby's gasping face,
 Or mother's bosom, or the rounded grace
   Of a girl's throat ; and what had seemed the red
   Of flowers was blood, in gouts and gushes shed
 From hearts that broke under that frolic pace.

And now and then from out the dreadful floor
  An arm or brow was lifted from the rest,
As if to strike in madness, or implore
  For mercy; and anon some suffering breast
Heaved from the mass and sank; and as before
  The revellers above them thronged and prest."

Mr. Howells has, indeed, learned rather late
in life a great fact which men, in general, ap-
prehend after a very few years of observation.
He has discovered that justice does not enter
into the scheme of our existence here. And
this is true. There is faith and there is truth,
there are charity and chastity and honesty, but
in all the world (speaking *more humano*) there
is no such thing as justice. And this discovery
startles and appalls him, for here again his individualism robs him of a sense of true proportion. It is the old New England trait, and it
must be admitted that in religion and philosophy it is almost universal among men, though
quite unreasoning and absurd. It is the conviction of the individual that in the great plan
of the universe he himself, his feelings, and his
fate are of some importance. Doubtless, for
instance, if Mr. Howells thinks that the narrative of his having given half a dollar to a beg-
gar is of sufficient interest to the world at large
to be preserved in several pages of printed text,

he also thinks that the question of his eternal
welfare attains an importance of inconceivable
vastness. But all this sort of feeling, so common in popular religious discussion, most curiously fails to recognize the infinite littleness of
the individual and of the world itself. There
are some who, giving law to the Deity, tell us
that the loss of a single soul would be a ca-
lamity so appalling as to be quite inconceivable; but in reality if all the men and women
who ever lived upon this earth and who ever
will inhabit it were swept into Gehenna at a
stroke, what would be the real importance of
it among the myriads of vigintillions of greater
and more glorious worlds that swarm amid the
infinity of space? Suppose that once upon a
time, thousands of years ago, in a far-dis-
tant quarter of our globe something once went
wrong with a mote in a sunbeam; this would
not be a very vital fact in the history of the
world. Yet it would really be relatively of far
more importance than, in its relation to the
whole infinite universe, would be the annihi-
lation of the mote of a world itself with all
the human atoms that breed and die upon it.
Why, even in his own country and among his
own kind, the individual does not count. Let
him be racked with pain or tortured by all the

agony that mind and body can endure, and if
he will but stand in his doorway he will see
the little children laughing in the sunshine
and hear the cackle of men and women to
whom he is not even so much as a name. Or,
like Iván Ilyitch, he may lie hopeless and alone,
watching his life ebb hourly away, and no one
will really care. His wife, who loves him and
whom he loves, will feel no more than a fleet-
ing sorrow; his child, whom he has watched
and cherished from its birth, will never understand his anguish; and both of them in the
end will half resent an affliction that acts as a
check upon their harmless pleasures. Nor can
the individual cry out against this as a wrong,
for God has willed it, and what He wills is
right.

The trouble with Mr. Howells is that he is a
pessimist who has as yet learned only the al-
phabet of pessimism. His eyes are opened to
the truth, yet he still hopes on, and hence is
torn with endless doubts. In speaking of one
author he says:

"While I read him I was in a world where right
came out best, as I believe it will yet do in this world;
and where merit was crowned with the success which
I believe will yet attend it in our daily life, untrammelled by economic circumstances."

But there can really be no permanent halt-
ing-place between optimism and pessimism ;
and he who, like Mr. Howells, is pessimistic
only up to a certain point lives in an inferno
of his own creation ; for he sees the evils of existence and is yet tormented by a hope that
never can be realized. Therefore, if one would
be at peace, he should be frankly either a consistent optimist or a profound pessimist ; for
it is a mistake to suppose that the pessimist is
unhappy. He is not. He is simply one who
has no illusions, and who has once for all accepted the inevitable. "He that is down need
fear no fall ;" and when we come to recognize
the fact that the very worst has happened to
us in being born, we can share the cheerful-
ness of him for whom this life has no surprises.
Nor, however dark the world may appear to
him, does he wish to leave it. His philosophy
is that of the sagacious Greek who taught with
great persuasiveness the doctrine that life is no
better than death, but who, when one of his
auditors asked him why, if life be no better
than death, he did not hasten to leave it, replied, "Because death is no better than life."

And, in fact, this is somewhat less than the
entire truth, for it is always possible that death
may be even worse than life. However firmly

we may hold to the teachings of religion, we
can never escape the feeling that haunted the
great Apostle to the Gentiles when he expressed the fear that even after he had done
everything he might still perchance become a
castaway.   One may live up to such light as
he possesses, yet he can never quite be sure
that his little all will be acceptable, or that
when the time arrives for the dissolution of
the ties that bind the body and the soul, the
sentient part of him may not be doomed to
go forth shuddering into infinite loneliness and
everlasting gloom.

Hence, the true pessimist is not concerned
with little things or with the multifarious evils
that he sees about him.   He knows that nothing can be done; that, suffer as he may, he
cannot help himself; and that in the universal
scheme it really doesn't matter.   Therefore
his mind is untrammelled by the cares and the
anxieties that beset his fellows.   If he hopes for
nothing, he also fears nothing, and he alone can
see the real unimportance of all human cares.
Physical pain may torture him, bereavement
may wring his heart and force from him a cry
of anguish; yet even then he can perceive the
underlying humor of it all, the uselessness of
complaint when one is spitted on the skewer

of destiny like a fly impaled upon a pin. So
he schools himself to patience, and strives to
acquire, not the sullen apathy of the Stoic,
but the splendid ataraxy that Epicurus taught.
Imbued with this, and knowing that whatever
may befall him there is nothing that can happen otherwise than God has willed it, he meets
the events of life with calm composure, looking upon them all with an unruffled front, and
with something of the divine serenity that
marks the life of the immortal gods.

In this short chapter, then, there have been
briefly indicated what seem to be the salient
points in the work of Mr. Howells—his artist-
ry, his power of delineation, his mastery of detail, and his unerring keenness of observation ;
and, on the other hand, the limitations that
arise from too great subtlety, from lack of ob-
jectivity, and from an imperfectly developed
philosophy of life. Were it within the scope
of this paper to dwell upon his personality,
much more might well be said; but it is unnecessary. Every one who knows his work
can feel how fine a nature lies behind it, how
much love of truth and justice, how much
charity, how much devotion to all that is best
and noblest; and every one who knows the
man himself can tell of his unassuming kindli-

ness, of his generosity to young writers who
have still their spurs to win, and of all the
traits that make his character so winning and
so truly typical of the high-minded American
gentleman.

MARCEL PRÉVOST

MARCEL PRÉVOST

M. MARCEL PRÉVOST is a very interesting
figure in the contemporaneous records of
French literature. Making his first appearance as an author only seven or eight years
ago with two not very successful books, he
has since then reached the position of a writer
whose popularity places him among the very
first of Parisian novelists. His books run into
forty, fifty, or sixty editions within a few
months of their first publication, and they
have at last become a topic of discussion in
England, where Mr. Andrew Lang has lately
been considering their author's merits ; while
the only productions of his that have as yet
been rendered into English have appeared in
this country within the past two years.

M. Prévost did not have long to wait for
critical recognition—a fact that in itself bears
striking testimony to the character of his literary workmanship ; for in a country where the
level of artistic excellence is so very high, and

where the critics, as a matter of duty, look
coldly upon the productions of a young and
aspiring writer who has still to show that he
possesses something more than superficial
cleverness and certain interesting tricks of
style, it is not easy to attract the serious
notice of a literary Rhadamanthus. M. Prévost's third novel, however, *Mlle. Jaufre*,
which appeared in 1890, gained at once the
attention of no less an authority than Jules
Lemaître, who praised the book most warmly
in his *Impressions Littéraires;* while *La Confession d'un Amant*, which was published in
the following year, broke through even the
austere reserve with which M. Ferdinand
Brunetière regards contemporary writers, and
forced from him a cautiously uttered though
very genuine note of admiration. *L'Automne
d'une Femme*, a subtle study of the woman
whose *grande passion* comes to her only after
the age of thirty years, deepened the impression made by its immediate predecessors.
Then followed M. Prévost's first great popular success in two volumes of short stories,
entitled respectively *Lettres de Femmes* and
Nouvelles Lettres de Femmes, which had an
immense and instantaneous vogue, as did a
somewhat similar collection entitled *Notre*

Compagne, whose fortieth edition was announced within three months after the volume first saw the light.

A writer who in eight short years has won
alike the commendation of the critics and the
attention of the public is certainly deserving
of some serious consideration. His own countrymen have compared him with George Sand
and with M. Paul Bourget; and there are, indeed, some striking points of close resemblance
in his work to that of these two writers; but
in each case the comparison, in part at least,
does something less than justice to M. Prévost. His style, indeed, has much in common
with the style of Mme. Dudevant. It has
her great facility and charm; and, too, her
literary watchward "idealize, idealize," is also
his, as he himself declared not very long ago;
but with him this fluency does not, as hers did,
pass into fluidity, while the touch of ideality is
never for an instant suffered to obscure that
clear impression of the actual which is as well
sustained by him as by the stoutest champions
of realism. For his conception of idealism
makes it to be not so much a thing apart from
real life and quite beyond it, as an essential
feature of that life itself. Thus, in a paper
on Romanticism, he asserts for the Romantic

a lasting place in the sum of human life, a
place in close association with the sphere of
the emotions, of the passions, and of the imagination. And in this he is far wiser than
Mr. Howells, for instance, who, while kindly
granting to the Romantic an actual existence
in our psychical and even in our material experience, does hold it to be so utterly exceptional as to rule it out of literary use and make
it only the rouge and raddle of a meretricious
art—a view of which, I think, each human life,
if fully known, could prove the falsity.

No less injustice is, in my opinion, done by
any hard and fast comparison of M. Prévost's
work with that of M. Paul Bourget. Both
writers are extremely psychological, but with
a difference. M. Bourget is psychological and
little else. His novels, while their exposition of conflicting motives is most curiously
keen, and while he can pursue it through all
its convolutions and tortuous complications,
are nevertheless, or rather for this very reason,
at times distinctly tedious. They often seem
almost to have the character of laboratory
demonstrations, and one's head often aches
as he labors through their fine-spun mazes
of analysis. But M. Prévost, while also very
subtle, does not make his psychological stud-

ies so portentous, nor spin them out to such a
grievous length.   He rather, by a few masterly and incisive touches, throws a vivid light
into the very heart of a situation, reveals as
by a flash a mental attitude, and thus accom-
plishes whatever M. Bourget can accomplish
with all his slow accumulation of detail.   It
may be that M. Bourget's psychology is more
profound ; but it is certain that M. Prévost's
is much better held in hand, and that his use
of it is far more consonant with literary art.
It helps, in other words, his purpose ; it does
not constitute that purpose.   It is with him a
means and not an end.

   In fact, if I were asked to name a modern
writer as being one to whom M. Prévost is in
his workmanship most closely kin, I should
unhesitatingly choose out Guy de Maupassant.
M. Prévost possesses the same swift, definite,
and unerring manner, the same compactness,
the same muscular grasp upon his material,
the same deft touch and lucid presentation.
Yet here, again, one must at once begin to
qualify.   In spite of a most striking superficial likeness, the spirit of the two is not
the same.   M. de Maupassant was saturated
with the joyless pessimism of modern France.
His cynical acceptance of the darkest side of

life as wholly normal, his torturing, agonizing
hopelessness, the moral gloom of his horizon,
the grim despair that, as one reads his work,
sink down upon the heart like an overpowering weight—all these are alien to the pages of
Marcel Prévost.   For he is not, in many of his
moods, a Frenchman of the modern school,
but rather a reversion to an earlier type, the
Frenchman of the sixteenth century, the *gail-
lard*, the gay adventurer, witty and gallant,
convinced that he is wholly irresistible, and
with a roguish eye wide open for some *bonne
fortune*.   This spirit is most clearly seen in his
short stories, than which no better illustration
of the *esprit Gaulois* can be found; and here
the temperamental contrast and also the sty-
listic likeness are most readily observed.   Nor
can one say, in opposition to this view, that
Maupassant has also lighter moods and even
moments of true tenderness, as shown respectively in *La Patronne*, that most audacious
story of a young *étudiant de droit*, and in *Le
Père de Simon*.   For the difference lies just
here: when Maupassant is simply droll or
simply tender, he is not really at his best,
while Prévost is.   The finest work of Maupassant is never seen in tales like these, but
in such bits of concentrated cynicism as *Un*

Sage and *Boule de Suif;* while Prévost's genius is most happy in those witty and ingenious
tales, of which *La Médaille* and *La Nuit de
Raymonde* are typical illustrations; and when
he takes a turn at cynicism he is distinctly ill
at ease and less artistic.

A critical comparison of the novels of the
two will lead one to the same conclusion.
Take, for example, Maupassant's powerful but
quite repulsive *Bel Ami* and read it side by
side with Prévost's *L'Automne d'une Femme.*
In *Bel Ami* is shown a world of absolute and
utter baseness, a world of prostitutes and
scoundrels. Not one of all its characters is
anything but vile, from the hero of the book
(a sorry hero) to the nymphomaniac Clotilde
de Marelle, and Mme. Walter, and her sly, pre-
cocious daughter Suzanne. This unrelieved
depravity, as Mr. Henry James has pointed
out, is really inartistic; for the very effect
which the writer apparently desires to produce would have been more strikingly attained had he availed himself of the aid of contrast and drawn his darkest figures on a lighter
background; and furthermore, the mind instinctively revolts from the inherent falsity
of such a picture, feeling at once that if mankind and womankind had really sunk so low as

this, society could not be held together for a
single day.

Far different is the moral and artistic attitude of M. Prévost in *L'Automne d'une Femme*.
It may be said that this fine novel, by far the
best its author has produced, is one whose
story is extremely sad; and this is true. But
sadness is a thing far different from horror
and despair; and neither horror nor despair
finds any place in the melancholy half-light of
this searching study. It tells, to summarize it
very briefly, of a charming and pure-minded
woman, Julie Surgère, married, or rather sold,
as a young girl to a repellent brute, who presently is stricken by a strange disease that makes
of him a living corpse. The years go on, and
at last the son of one of her husband's part-
ners, Maurice Artoy, a young man, crosses her
path. She nurses him through an illness, and in-
sensibly drifts into a tender and self-sacrificing
love for him, a love that is her first. But she is
much older than he, and in time he is attracted
by the fresher beauty of a young girl, Claire
Esquier, the daughter of another partner, and
an inmate of her own home. The elder woman, who is fond of Claire, and who sees that
Maurice every day is growing colder, renounces
him and all her dreams of happiness, and lets

him marry her unconscious rival, while she
herself suffers in silence and looks forward to
a life of sorrow and self-abnegation. The
treatment of this theme is the antithesis of
anything that can be found in Maupassant.
The hero of the book, Maurice Artoy, is, to
be sure, as disagreeable as any of Maupassant's
creations. He is a sentimental sensualist, and,
if possible, is more repulsive even than Georges
Duroy in *Bel Ami*—Duroy the thorough-paced
blackguard, the sublimation of a type that finds
its genesis in the *maquereau* of the Faubourg
St. Antoine. But Artoy's baseness and his
selfishness serve only to bring out in strong
relief the truth and beauty of the other characters—of Claire, the innocent young girl, her
father Jean Esquier, the soul of honor and fidelity, and Julie Surgère herself, loving wrong-
fully, indeed, but with a love which is more
than half maternal, and whose sacrifice con-
signs her to a life of sorrow that expiates her
fault. There is passion here, and there is sin;
but there are also remorse and repentance
and an infinite tenderness. Nothing could be
more admirable than the self-restraint with
which M. Prévost has managed the development of the theme, and nothing more delicate
than the art that finds expression in this novel,

which as the study of a love outworn need not
avoid comparison with George Sand's great
masterpiece, *Lucrezia Floriani.*

From what has now been said it can be
readily inferred what are the leading qualities
that give M. Prévost his marked distinction: a
nearly perfect style, a very subtle insight into
all the workings of the human mind, and a
touch of ideality that differentiates his work
from that of the uncompromising realists who
ignore the one thing that is wanting to breathe
life into their creations and make them truly
vital and convincing. His minor literary virtues are equally conspicuous. Some one has
said of the modern pessimistic school in fiction, whose foremost representative to-day is
Gabriele D'Annunzio, that they are afraid to
be amusing; and to this generalization M.
Prévost is a most agreeable exception. A
rare and irresistible drollery abounds in nearly
all his lesser fiction ; and even his most cynical
tales are lightened and relieved by a brilliant
wit that is very far to seek in most of his contemporaries. His ingenuity and intellectual
dexterity are also most surprising; so that
one's breath is often taken quite away by the
unexpectedness and audacity of his invention.
Sometimes, again, he touches on the sphere of

the mysterious and occult, and then his art recalls the art of Poe, as in *La Demoiselle au
Chat d'Or*, a curiously weird conception whose
power is enhanced by the simplicity and restraint of the form in which the narrative is
cast.

It must, of course, be understood that what
has just been said of M. Prévost's work is
said of what is best in all that work. He
has undoubtedly at times sunk far below his
higher level, and has put his name to things
that bear the marks of unadulterated mediocrity. Two general criticisms have been lev-
elled at him and may very briefly be considered here. The first is one that equally applies
to Maupassant and many others of the writers
of French fiction. The very French and, to
an Anglo-Saxon mind, unpardonable freedom
that he often gives himself in his selection of
a theme, makes many of his works, and nearly
all his shorter stories, quite impossible for any
but a Frenchman to admire without a qualm.
With him the *conte leste* touches on the very
limits of audacity and unreserve; and even the
most hardened reader of contemporary continental fiction is sometimes startled by the unexpected daring of his fancy.

Yet this much may at least be said in his

behalf. He never, like M. de Maupassant,
descends to any coarseness or offensiveness
of phrase, but writes invariably in language
whose discretion and extraordinary delicacy
in part redeem his subject from that grossness
and offensiveness which in the hands of any
purely naturalistic writer it would certainly
possess. In all that he has published, not a
single page exists so thoroughly detestable as
Maupassant's *La Femme de Paul*, of which the
hideous brutality is fitly matched by its inartistic crudity of treatment. In Prévost's little
story called *Au Cabaret* the same theme is just
touched upon, yet the difference in the hand-
ling is remarkable. The underlying thought
is one that no Anglo-Saxon would ever for a
moment dream of using as the basis of a story;
but in Prévost's hands it is a mere suggestion
rather than a boldly voiced *motif;* and the
tale itself, in spite of its essential impropriety,
leaves on the mind no lingering taint, but
rather, by the artful use of contrast, a strong
impression of the power of innocence and of
the lurking good that lingers somewhere even
in the loathliest. And so in all his work there
can be found a glimpse, a hint, of something
better, a certain humanity and warmth that
save the writer and the reader, too, from an

unmitigated cynicism. Nor should one fail to note that some of his most perfect writing is morally impeccable. He has written several short stories that are as pure in thought as they are exquisite in literary finish, and these display, as in a drop of crystal, all his finest gifts—his power of compression, his unerring insight into character, his humor, his sympathy, and his moving pathos.

Besides the censure of the moralist, however, M. Prévost has often had to meet another criticism which, from the artistic point of view, is far more serious. Not long ago I said to a distinguished critic who had spoken rather slightingly of Prévost's work:

"What is the real reason for your prejudice against Prévost? Why will you not admit his right to rank with Maupassant?"

And he replied:

"Because I feel that Maupassant is quite sincere and that Prévost is not."

This confident assertion of his "insincerity" is rather common among the critics of Prévost, though less, I think, in France than in this country, where it has almost become a formula. It rests, in my opinion, wholly on a desultory and imperfect knowledge of his writings. In the case of the critic who has just been quoted, a

5

further conversation showed that he had never
read a single one of Prévost's longer novels,
nor even all his shorter stories; and he very
frankly said that his opinion was largely the
result of some casual conversation with Prévost himself. How thoroughly unfair is any
judgment formed in such a fashion, one scarcely needs to say. As a matter of fact, this un-
favorable opinion in general is chiefly due to
the bad impression produced by a single novel
of Prévost's, *Les Demi-Vierges*. It is, indeed,
unfortunate that of all his writings this was
the first to be rendered into English. It is still
more unfortunate that he ever wrote it at all,
for it is entirely unworthy of his genius. A
bit of pure sensationalism and distorted psychology, untrue to life and quite offensive in
its treatment, it shows the writer at his very
worst, and strikes a thoroughly discordant
note. Whoever judges him by this may readily be pardoned for ranking him with writers
like Adolphe Belot and Paul Ginisty; but
surely no serious criticism of a literary artist
ought ever to be made to rest upon the reading of a single book.

Le Jardin Secret, the latest novel that M.
Prévost has written, has a very special interest. Of all his works this is the one that from

the very moment of its publication met a perfectly respectful treatment at the critics' hands,
and it may, I think, be styled one of the most
important works of fiction that the French
have lately given us. It had in France, of
course, the great advantage of being the first
long novel written by its author since his literary gifts were generally recognized; but quite
apart from this, it well deserves a careful study:
and I think that from some points of view its
interest is even greater for an English or an
American reader than for the fellow-country-
men of its creator.

Its story is narrated by one Mme. Marthe
Lecoudrier, who is its central figure. She is
the wife of Jean Lecoudrier, the head of a department in a banking-house, Le Crédit Commercial, and hence the story has to do with
the life and the environment of the *bourgeoisie
médiocre*. At the commencement of the novel,
M. Lecoudrier has left her for a few days' visit
to his early home, Ingrandes, where his uncle
has just died and willed him a small property.
The wife, sitting alone throughout the evening in her apartment, with her little daughter
sleeping quietly in an adjoining room, falls
into a reminiscent mood, and for the first time
in many years begins to summon up the recol-

lections of her girlhood, of *la Marthe d'au-
trefois*, a girl ambitious, eager for a brilliant
career, hopeful of a literary, and ultimately
of a social, triumph.   As she recalls her past,
she smiles at the contrast afforded by her present life, the life of a *bonne bourgeoise*, satisfied
with a humdrum existence and with long, un-
eventful days of peace and commonplace contentment.   Presently her eye falls upon a drawer of her husband's desk from which a bunch of
keys projects. Without much purpose she opens
it and half mechanically turns over a packet of
papers which the drawer contains.   At once her
attention is arrested.   With a beating heart
she unties the packet and finds in it the evidence of a secret whose existence she had
never dreamed of.   It holds a number of pho-
tographs, a bunch of artificial flowers from a
woman's hat, letters signed with the names
of women quite unknown to her, a child's portrait, and finally a bundle of government se-
curities to the value of thirty thousand francs
or more, from which the coupons have been
regularly cut. A careful reading of the letters
and an examination of the other articles lead
her irresistibly to certain definite conclusions:
that her husband has been for years untrue to
her, that he has somewhere another child, and

that unknown to her he has set apart a sum of
money whose income is devoted to the pur-
poses of the other life that he has lived apart
from her. But there is even more to be inferred than this. A number of letters from
Ingrandes, written apparently by a confidential servant, give her reasons for believing that
her husband's family is one afflicted by a tendency to epilepsy; and she recalls with a thrill
of horror certain mysterious seizures that he
has sometimes suffered from, and that have
once or twice already appeared in her own
young child. Her heart dies within her as
she sits down to consider the revelation that
has come to her. She has been deceived in
every possible way in which a woman can be
duped, and for the moment she is stunned.
A terrible feeling of despair comes over her,
followed by a flaming fever of indignation.
Yet may she not be quite mistaken? May
there not be, after all, an explanation possible that will be consistent with her husband's truth and constancy? When morning
comes she hurries to an agency which gives
*renseignements intimes particuliers dans l'in-
térêt des familles*—in other words, a sort of
private detective bureau. To its chief she
confides the compromising packet and asks

for *informations discrètes*.   An immediate and
absolute divorce is in her mind, and she waits
in a state of almost unendurable impatience
for the confirmation of the apparent facts, and
for the evidence that will set her free from a
man so stained with treachery.   For the moment a dumb, helpless rage inspires her—a
passionate longing for revenge.   Soon, however, when another day has dragged along, a
strong reaction comes upon her, a physical
lassitude, a sort of moral cowardice resulting
from an exhausting waste of energy.

" I feel like letting everything just go, without taking the trouble to set matters right, without saying a
word to my husband, without doing a single thing.
. . . For a woman nearly forty years of age to leave
her home like one of Ibsen's heroines, just because
she has been deceived—this really seems to me, at
three o'clock in the afternoon, somewhat absurd.   For
the first time I consider the question of remaining,
with all the conscious superiority which my knowledge of Jean's secrets would give me—remaining, in
fact, for my revenge.   A sort of nerveless indecision
has got hold of me.   The thing is wholly in my hands
—the household need not be upset; nothing need be
changed in what Goethe's Egmont calls ' the amicable
habits of one's life.'   And, after all, this life with Jean
would be endurable."

For the first time she begins to realize how

wonderfully close, how almost irrefragable are
the ties which years of married life can weave;
how all the little incidents and intimacies of
the home, the myriad interests that man and
wife possess in common, the very sight of one
another day after day for years, establish a
powerful habit, and constitute a bond almost
impossible to break.

" And, therefore, even the association of two beings
who are quite indifferent to one another may come to
be with the help of time an affectionate and lasting
union of two souls united in reality. . . . For it is not
the words of the marriage service that constitute the
essence of true marriage, nor is it even mutual love,
when that exists; for words are only of the lips, and
love may really be the negation of a marriage. A
man and a woman are truly married only when they
have become, through the influence of their life together, *kindred*, as when two persons are allied by
blood. When the wife has become to the husband
that sister of whom the Canticle makes mention, then
only is the marriage truly consummated. This mystical process lies in a gradual transformation, of which
neither of the pair has any consciousness until it has
been actually wrought. No matter, then, how the
laws may at any future time transform and modify its
legal basis, so long as the life together and the community of interests remain, for just so long will marriage, as we understand it now, continue to exist."

Nevertheless, she gets from the detective

bureau facts which show that all her fears are
true ; that all her wrongs are very real; and
they include names and dates and information
as to places which make all further doubt impossible. But in the meantime something else
has come to her. The reminiscent mood that
had begun upon the very evening of her terrible discovery returns. In judging her husband
and condemning him as false to her, she calls
to mind her own past years of life. She knows
his secrets ; she has entered into that retreat
which he had thought secure against invasion.
But has she not herself some carefully seclud-
ed *jardin secret* of memory which, could he
likewise enter, he would find as eloquent of
treachery to him ? The question deeply moves
her, and her secret consciousness makes her
shrink and shudder at the thought. Can she
pronounce a judgment upon him and be herself quite free from condemnation ? She meets
the question, at first evasively, and at last un-
flinchingly. She will summon up her past and
judge it just as mercilessly as she judged her
husband's.

She goes back to her years of girlhood and
its varied incidents. She remembers how her
father, a *chef de gare*, had misappropriated
money to waste it at the gaming - table and

in other forms of dissipation. She brings to
mind his pitiful disgrace, his conviction and
imprisonment as a felon, her later years of
shabbiness and squalor. She recalls how, after he had died, she had become a sort of gov-
erness, and then had met in her employer's
family the son of a rich Belgian manufacturer
and had loved him. She thinks once more of
how she used to meet him secretly, and how
these meetings, though quite innocent, were
broken off when he was ordered by his parents
to end the undesirable entanglement, and how
her lover had obeyed because he feared to
jeopardize for a woman's sake his hope of fortune. She thinks of how, when she was still
tormented by the agony and shame of this re-
jection, a lady who was interested in her had
proposed to bring about her marriage with M.
Lecoudrier, whom she had never met, and of
whom she knew no more than that he was reported fairly prosperous and of good repute.
After a meeting or two she had accepted him,
and a *mariage de convenance* had been arranged.

Her mind reverts to her thirteen years of
married life. She remembers how, at first, the
novelty of her surroundings, the comparative
ease of her environment, her pleasure in being
mistress of her husband's house and in the

kindness and consideration with which he always treated her, had satisfied her mind and
gradually tranquillized her. The birth of a
daughter had bound her still more closely to
her husband.   But there came a time when all
these things had palled upon her, when her
home and all its duties had become unspeak-
ably monotonous, when even her child had
ceased to interest her, and when the prospect
of a humdrum life of *bourgeois* dulness had become intolerable.   Her old-time restlessness
and craving for excitement were again awak-
ened, and their satisfaction took the form of
gallantry. She recalls how she began to accept
and even seek the notice of those men about
her who were young and easily *toqués*.   Then
came a period of flirtation, of sentimental
friendships such as certain types of men and
women frequently affect—professedly Platonic
liaisons in which the vocabulary of friendship
is consciously substituted for the language of
love, and in which the pressure of hands, the
solitude à deux, and the *valse significative* play
an important part.   But as Platonic friendships
seldom fill up all the blanks in the *carte tendre*
of a woman's life, it was not long before a much
more serious affair occurred, when a certain
Captain Landouzie became a frequent visitor

in her drawing-room. This person, representing *le type buffle*—forceful, violent, and a good deal of a brute—was the sort of man who always has a singular attraction for women of the sensitive, imaginative, half-neurotic temperament, who seem to find in the presence of a nature so completely physical something that rests their nerves and roughly overrides their finical hesitations. And it was so in this case; for, as she now remembers but too well, in no long time Landouzie had completely dominated Marthe Lecoudrier; and she was saved from taking the final step only by an unexpected incident that called him hastily to join his regiment. A long and serious illness followed; and at its end her period of storm and stress was over. From that time down to the discovery of her husband's secret she had lived contentedly the life that once had seemed quite unendurable.

She thinks of all these episodes, and as she thinks of them she feels that it is not for her to sit in judgment on her husband. She took him in the beginning without asking any questions, just as he took her. If he concealed the physical taint that rested on his race, so had she equally concealed the social taint that her father's crime had fastened on herself. If her

husband came to her with the memory of other
loves in mind, so had she come to him distracted by the loss of the only man she ever cared
for, and one of whom the recollection still
made any thought of marriage with another
seem detestable. Her husband had professed
no love for her, and she had equally professed
no love for him. And after marriage, if she
now knew that he had not lived for her alone,
her conscience told her that she had not truly
lived for him; and that while she had never
actually broken any vows as he had done, she
still was morally as bad as he, since circumstances, rather than her will, had saved her.
Recalling all her past and weighing it against
his secret, she hesitates no more. His faults
are balanced by her own, and henceforth she
will banish both forever from her memory and
live with this thought always in her mind,
that " from to-day, and only from to-day, I am
in very truth a *wife*."

Such is the outline of the story upon which
Marcel Prévost has built his latest novel. So
far as it possesses any moral, it appears to be
intended to assert that every woman of thirty
years of age or more who will look carefully
into the souvenirs of her past, will find among
the fruits of her experience quite enough to

make her charitable in her judgment of the
other sex who have temptations such as she
is largely shielded from. To this assertion
many readers will very naturally demur; and
as for M. Prévost's view that every human
being, man or woman, has his or her *jardin
secret*, this thought is hardly new enough to
justify the writing of a novel to expound it;
for, indeed, it was set forth by Thackeray
many years ago in one of his most striking
passages. The interest of the book for M.
Prévost's countrymen is, therefore, probably to
be found in the skill and subtlety of its literary
workmanship and in the innumerable touches
that show so rare an understanding of the
working of a woman's mind.

But to the American and the English reader this novel has an interest of a very different
sort. These will perceive in it not only an entertaining story, a work of literary charm, another lucid and elaborate study of the *ewig
Weibliche;* but, more than this, a document
containing very valuable evidence as to the
physiological and psychic basis of the *mariage
de convenance.* Than this there is perhaps no
social institution that more deeply interests
the Anglo-Saxon student of French manners,
as there is none more utterly at variance with

'Anglo - Saxon sentiment and prejudice. To
find a keen observer, therefore, like M. Prévost, unconsciously affording us so accurate a
demonstration of its practical results, is marvellously interesting ; nor should one pass over
this demonstration without at least a general
indication of what seems to be its obvious
teaching.

The French assert, in explaining and defending their peculiar institution, that in the long
run the happiness of marriage depends far
more upon material considerations and upon
environment than upon an actual affinity of
two persons at the time of marriage. Given
any conceivable amount of love between the
two, this still must wane in time ; and sooner
or later the union must rest upon a different
basis from that of sentiment alone. Therefore,
in the *mariage de convenance*, this basis is most
carefully arranged beforehand by the family
council, viewing with practical and unromantic
eyes the permanent interests of both the prin-
cipals. It is essential, for example, that they
should be of equal, or of nearly equal, social
rank ; that there should be no great disparity
in age ; that character and temperament should
be considered ; and that the united incomes of
the two should be sufficient to assure them all

the comforts to which they have been hitherto
accustomed, and to guarantee a suitable provision for the presumptive responsibilities of the
future. A second proposition which relates to
the sentimental side of marriage is accepted as
essentially complemental to the first. As love
is, in its very last analysis, held to be a purely
physical affair, and as it is inspired by mere
proximity, its evocation may be safely counted
on as an inevitable incident of any properly
considered marriage. That is to say, if the
young girl be educated in seclusion, so that no
attachment for another has come to her before
her marriage, the purely emotional side of her
nature will at marriage be still a *tabula rasa*, a
fair white page, on which her husband may in-
scribe his name and win the affection which
among ill-regulated Teutonic peoples he seeks
to do as a preliminary to betrothal. Then,
when in course of time the married pair adjust
themselves to the relation that is to end at
death alone, the wife has no remembrance of
any other attachment to impair a single-minded interest in her husband; and with a comfortable environment and an assured provision,
both go through life's long journey hand-in-
hand, unvexed by unforeseen anxieties, serene
and confident, and with that complete tran-

quillity which is the most secure of all foundations for mutual affection and esteem. The
scheme is beautifully logical ; it possesses the
lucidity, completeness, and simplicity that are
so characteristic of all French theory; it is
based upon that intensely material view of
life which in France has come to be a national
possession ; and it has about it something of
the impenetrable hardness which, with all their
superficial sentiment, remains the one eternal-
ly and profoundly significant trait that under-
lies French character.

But the Anglo-Saxon, who is never infatu-
ated with any theory whatever merely because
it is logical and lucid, and who has a most uncomfortable way of looking at its practical application, entertains some definite objections
to this view of marriage ; and two of these may
be restated here, because this book of M. Prévost seems to shed some light upon the questions they involve. Assuming (which is a good
deal to assume) that these businesslike and
scientific marriages are really so extremely
well arranged that women are never sacrificed
to brutes, and that men are never tricked into a
union with women whom they would not think
of choosing for themselves, what is the actual
relation of all these arrangements to the wom-

an's happiness?   When a young and innocent
girl, brought up in a conventual seclusion, is
handed over to a man whom she has scarcely
ever seen and for whom she can have no particular prepossession, what, one may ask, are
probably her feelings?   It may be true, as Mr.
Howells very delicately puts it, that man is
still imperfectly monogamous ; but it is also
true that woman is essentially monandrous ;
and this implies the right of choice, since it is
a negation of the masculine promiscuity. Does
she then, in fact, so very readily adjust herself
to a situation which to her is quite unique ?
Does she not, when roughly thrust into the
intimacy of married life, feel a revolt so strong
as to make her husband more or less an object
of repulsion to her?   This very natural inquiry
gets a sort of answer from M. Prévost. I give
his dictum in the very words that he has placed
in the mouth of Marthe Lecoudrier :

"Comment font toutes les autres, qui n'ont même
pas cette aide, petites bourgeoises quelconques que
l'on marie comme on m'a mariée ? Passent-elles outre
les répugnances, grâce à leur naturelle inertie, à une
vague et bestiale curiosité, ou simplement au désir
niais d'avoir un ménage, d'être ' Madame '?   Au fond,
je crois que chez beaucoup de jeunes filles la peur de
l'homme inconnu n'est pas telle que le bruit en court,

6

et que se l'imagine le petit nombre de celles que rési-
dent au sommet de l'échelle des êtres sensitifs. Beaucoup de jeunes filles n'ont aucune vraie pudeur. La
pudeur leur est apprise, suggérée, comme un principe
de sage économie générale : à savoir, qu'une femme
perd un avantage à se donner. Mais elles n'éprouvent
nulle gêne à s'étendre à côté d'un homme, du moment
que la perte est régulièrement compensée, que l'usage
social est respecté, qu'elles-mêmes sont sûres de faire
'comme tout le monde.'. . . Oui, il faut l'avouer !
ces pauvres raisons suffisent à l'immense majorité
des jeunes épouses ! On fait ' comme tout le monde,'
dans une circonstance où la vraie noblesse d'âme com-
manderait de faire comme soi-même, comme soi seul."

This surely is a very cynical defence, for it
resolves itself into an expansion of the famous
line of Pope that "every woman is at heart a
rake," a saying which, by the way, was not
original with Pope, but was drawn by him
from a quite Gallic epigram of Jehan de
Meung. Yet M. Prévost thoroughly believes
in it ; for in this very novel his account of the
early days of the Lecoudriers' *lune de miel* is
but a concrete illustration of the same idea,
recalling an extremely curious passage in
Gautier's *Mademoiselle de Maupin*, where that
adventurous young woman in her male dis-
guise spends the first night of her freedom in
a rustic inn. The Anglo-Saxon, with his great-

er reverence for women, will not find such an apologia conclusive.

But something far more subtle and more vitally important still remains. M. Prévost depicts his heroine when, by the accepted theory of the *mariage de convenance*, she should have reached the period of tranquillity, as a true *bourgeoise soumise*, suddenly becoming restless, bored, *ennuyée*, eager for excitement, and ready to seek it elsewhere than at home. Why is this so? It seems to vitiate the principle laid down by all the social philosophers who defend the view of marriage which prevails in France. M. Prévost explains it by a reference to what he styles *la crise*. Again I give his very words:

"Il y a un moment où une femme qui jusque-là a été satisfaite par le mariage, arrive à souhaiter autre chose. . . . Quand le régime conjugal est enfin établi, quand l'accoutumance est complète, aussitôt l'épouse sent que ce trouble délicieux, ce trouble antérieur lui manque. Regret du passé chez l'honnête femme, désir de l'aventure chez les autres ; combien éprouvent le besoin d'un *nouveau mariage*, où tout ce qu'il y eut d'exquis dans la première initiation se recommence !"

These very frank statements will seem to the Anglo-Saxon reader an unconscious condem-

nation of the whole theory of marriage which
prevails in France, and to support by implica-
tion the Teutonic view.   For the Teutonic
view assumes that the love on which alone a
happy marriage can be based, so far from being allied solely with the senses, is a far more
spiritual thing—an exaltation arising, first of
all, from certain psychical affinities between
two persons whose temperament exactly fits
them for each other.   It has in it, on the one
side, an element of maternal affection, and on
the other something of the self-devotion and
disinterestedness involved in ties of blood re-
lationship.   It cannot be called forth indiffer-
ently by one person as well as by another, but
must spring from an instinctive recognition of
the subtle fitness of two natures for each other; and it is based, therefore, upon that principle of selection which is one of the most
profound and universal of all natural laws.
When, moreover, it is thus evoked, it so completely moulds and masters every faculty of
mind and body as to preclude the possibility
of any other similar and coexistent sentiment.
In its fullest and most perfect evocation it appears but once in any human life; and that it
should be thus permitted to appear is both a
physiological and a psychological necessity.

The nature that through special circumstances
has never known it has been cheated of its
rights; and the whole being, whether consciously or unconsciously, will sooner or later
rise up in revolt. Thus, as M. Huysmans in
En Route declares (and I have heard the statement vouched for by very eminent ecclesias-
tics of the Catholic Church), even in the cloister
there comes a time in the life of the most devoted *religieuse* when she finds with dismay
that her existence is becoming quite intolerable, when her best-loved duties fail to interest her, and when a mysterious lassitude creeps
over mind and body. She, in her innocence and
inexperience, does not understand its meaning,
but her superiors do. They know it to be the
crise, the mighty instinct of womanhood crying
out within her, and they dread the outcome;
for with many nuns it assumes the form of
physical decline and ends in early death.

Now, in the *mariage de convenance*, which
takes into account the physiological phase
alone, and disregards a very vital psychic
truth, the *crise* still lingers in the background
to be reckoned with hereafter. It has not necessarily been coincident with marriage, but it
may still occur at any time to overturn the
scientifically accurate arrangements of the *con-*

seil de famille and to provide the writers of
French fiction with the particular sort of incident which forms the staple of their literary
studies. In the Teutonic marriage, on the
other hand, the *crise* is not a factor in the later
matrimonial problem, for it has been synchronous with the marriage rite. Nature, which is
mightier than Art, has had her due ; and henceforth there exists in the mind of the wife no
lingering dissatisfaction, no vaguely curious
yearning after what M. Prévost calls *l'homme
providentiel.* The basis for a lasting sympathy
has been securely laid ; and man and wife live
out their days together, bound fast by ties that
do not gall, and that are infinitely stronger than
those imposed in selfish bargaining and nice
consideration of the *dot*—by ties, in fact, which
will survive external shock, and which adver-
sity itself will only knit more closely in bringing out through sacrifice of self the pure devotion and eternal tenderness that blend two
hearts in one and constitute the sacramental
mystery of marriage.

GEORGE MOORE

GEORGE MOORE

A YEAR or two ago M. Émile Zola made a
sort of pilgrimage to London, and was there
received with the overwhelming and indiscrim-
inate attention which the English always give
to the latest lion, whether he be a great bene-
factor of the human race or a King of the Can-
nibal Islands. Foremost among the throng
that hastened to welcome the distinguished
exponent of naturalism was observed a learned
judge who, only a short time before, had sent
a publisher to prison for issuing an English
version of one of M. Zola's works ; and this circumstance was very naturally taken as a text
by the Continental press for sermons anent
the hypocrisy and insincerity of the British
nation. A perusal of the books produced of
late by Mr. George Moore gives rise to somewhat similar reflections.

Ten years ago, Mr. Moore's first great success, *A Mummer's Wife*, was the talk of literary London, and was sending thrills of horror

down the spines of the Philistines. It was
cast out of Mudie's as unfit for any one's perusal. The fiat of Mr. W. H. Smith excluded
it from all the news-stalls. Mr. Moore was
banned and badgered by the unco' guid, and
even by many who made no special claim to
virtue. To-day he is spoken of with marked
respect as a bold, original, and powerful writer
whose work deserves most serious study; and,
in fact, his latest volumes come, not from the
ill-starred press that first exploited him, nor
from the neutral house that afterwards accepted books of his; but they show upon the title-
page an imprint that bears with it not only re-
spectability, but distinction.

Yet Mr. Moore himself has undergone no
change in any way since the time when he
was so bitterly denounced; nor has his theory
of art been changed. He is quite as pessimistic as he ever was. His plots reek quite as
strongly as they ever did of adultery, and drink,
and despair. Why is he now *persona grata* to
the publishers, and the libraries, and the critics?
The fact is, that the treatment accorded to M.
Zola and Mr. Vizetelly, and to the George
Moore of ten years ago, and that which this
same novelist receives to-day, are not in reality
symptomatic of British hypocrisy, but rather

of British inconsistency, an inconsistency that comes from jumbling together two utterly irreconcilable motives—the artistic motive and the motive of morality. At one time the latter gets control, and Mr. Moore is damned; at another the artistic sentiment is in the ascendant, and he is set upon a throne in a sort of apotheosis. Now, as a matter of fact, either point of view is quite defensible. It hardly admits of question that *A Mummer's Wife* and *Mike Fletcher*—yes, and *Esther Waters* and *Celibates*—are very far from being the sort of reading that one would recommend *virginibus puerisque.* Personally, I do not think their tendency to be immoral, but the contrary, because they paint vice in such ghastly colors; yet the knowledge of vice which they display is hardly edifying. On the other hand, it is quite as fair to judge them wholly on their literary merits, and thus to speak of them in the very warmest terms of praise. In England, however, the motive of morality is forever clashing with the purely artistic instinct, thus leading in practice to the paradoxical result described above.

Mr. Moore is unique among English writers of to-day. An Irishman by birth, he received his training in Paris, where he lived so long as almost to lose the idiomatic command of his mother-tongue, a fact recorded by himself in his interesting *Confessions of a Young Man;* and his first novel, a story of Ireland under the Land League, was actually written and published in French. Returning to England, however, he recovered his use of literary English, and after a series of somewhat desultory experiments, began to contribute regularly to the pages of those ephemeral publications that are seldom seen outside of London, and that in London find their limited circulation within the borders of literary and artistic Bohemia. Mr. Moore wrote much and often—dramatic criticisms, art criticism, literary criticism—developing a style and an intellectual purpose that have become very distinctive in his later and more ambitious work. He put forth also several fugitive attempts at fiction, until at last he gave to the world a novel which still remains the best known as well as the most striking thing that he has done.

A Mummer's Wife narrates the story of a woman of the lower middle class, one reared in the strictest, narrowest fashion known to the English of the provincial towns, but one whose temperament is crossed by sensuous impulses that lie dormant in her early life, because nothing has occurred as yet to waken them. So she lives on with her feeble, asthmatic husband, keeping his shop for him and eking out their income by her needle. She is a woman of much physical attractiveness, and when, one day, the manager of a travelling dramatic troupe becomes a lodger in the house, he immediately lays siege to her, and with ultimate success; so that she leaves her husband for her lover and with him enters on a life whose novel freedom and tawdry Bohemianism fascinate her, especially when she finally becomes herself a player and enters fully into the nomadic, happy-go-lucky, lawless existence of her new companions. The story that follows is a curious study of the general deterioration of her character — of a pathetic and unceasing struggle between the enduring constraint of heredity and of her early training, and the powerful influences with which her new environment appeals to those subtly interwoven traits that thrill her whole being in answer to their urgings. She is *une âme désorientée*, distracted, unbalanced; and the exposition of the process by which she slowly sinks to the very lowest depths of degradation is powerful, and pitiless, and searching. With one exception Mr. Moore has never done such perfect character-drawing as in this book, which contains a dozen men and women who are marvellously realized. Dick Lennox, the actor-lover, fat, vulgar, "sensual as a mutton-chop," absolutely devoid of sentiment, yet absolutely honest, and good-natured to the verge of weakness, is a remarkable study, and so is Kate herself in every stage of her career, from the first pages of the book, where we find her primly waiting in the shop, to the crisis, where at the death of her infant she takes to drink, and at the end, where she is wallowing in the gutters, wrecked in hope, enfeebled in intellect, and lost to shame. Intensely vivid is the minutely curious picture of the life of the strolling players, their intrigues, their quarrels, their shady, shifty, hand-to-mouth devices, their conceit, their comradeship, their paltry triumphs, and their squalid troubles. No less remarkable is the carefully drawn study of the development of the drink-habit in a woman who fights against it and endeavors to conceal its progress with all the subtlety of deceit of which the drunkard and the opium - eater alone are capable.

The vogue of *A Mummer's Wife*, which, thanks partly to the advertising given it by those who tried to secure its practical sup-

pression, passed to its fourteenth edition in
the first year of its publication, won for Mr.
Moore's succeeding novels an instant hearing.
And they well deserved it; for, in spite of many
and obvious defects and inequalities, they were
original and strong, and they represented besides a particular literary *genre* that had had
as yet no representative in English. Of these
further works *A Modern Lover* is a novel of
the world of art, its central figure being one
of those effeminate, corrupt, deceitful natures
so frequently found in men who follow the
artistic career, and who for some not very
obvious reason exercise a curious fascination
upon women. Seymour, the artist in question, is wholly base, yet through his power over
women, whom he systematically uses and de-
ceives, he makes his way successfully from
poverty to social and professional success.
Vain Fortune, the least interesting of anything
that Mr. Moore has done, is a study of femi-
nine jealousy, skilfully conceived and firmly
drawn, but rather slight and lacking in perspective. *A Drama in Muslin* was written as
an attempt to draw the modern girl as shown
in three distinct and different types, so that in
this book men play no very important part;
but as a study in temperament the attempt

is scarcely a success.　One gets an impression
of nothing very characteristic, and certainly of
nothing that may be taken as being really
typical.　Yet in another way the book is one
of some importance.　The scene is laid in
Ireland, and the life depicted is that of the
"Castle set"—the half-impoverished gentry
and those who wish to be considered as among
the gentry.　To the future social historian of
Britain this novel may well prove an interesting document; for Mr. Moore knows his
ground most thoroughly, and he has caught
to perfection the squalid, frowzy setting and
the scarcely subdued vulgarity of that mori-
bund society which in another generation will
be happily extinct.

As *A Drama in Muslin* was written to describe the typical young woman, *Mike Fletcher*
—a novel, by the way, whose title is said to
have very materially hurt its sale—embodies
Mr. Moore's conception of the men who are
typical of our time.　One would be very sorry, however, to accept the personages of this
book as being any but sporadic specimens.
At the most they can only typify the London
"bounder" in several of his most unpleasant
phases; nor have they any real importance to
readers whose lives are lived a hundred miles

from Leicester Square and Piccadilly Circus
and the Strand. They are all more or less
young, they are chiefly bachelors living in
chambers in the Temple, or in contiguous
lodgings. Some of them are journalists and
some are artists and some are merely men-
about-town ; but all of them alike devote their
days and nights to wine and women and riot
and brawling, with intervals of erotic verse-
writing, and rather incoherent philosophical
discussions punctuated with stupid jokes and
ribald stories. Mike Fletcher himself, the un-
savory hero of the book, who is described in
its pages by one of his admirers as a "toff,"
is a thorough-going cad, the son of an Irish
peasant, who gets on after a fashion by a combination of impudence and subserviency, and
whose success with women of every class is as
great as that of Seymour in *A Modern Lover*.
But Mike Fletcher, after inheriting a fortune
from one of these impressionable beings and
after having exhausted every possible form of
what he views as pleasure, is haunted by a
Weltschmerz so profound and so unconquer-
able that in the end he takes his own life
after a most ghastly scene of hopeless, horrifying self-communion. The book is in a way a
powerful one, and some of its episodes are

7

very striking; but in writing it Mr. Moore did
not have all of his material quite thoroughly
in hand. The story is not compact, but is too
often vague; and he resorts now and then
to improbabilities, as when he makes Mike
Fletcher rush off to the desert in a moment
of boredom and become the chosen friend of
an Arab chief among the Bedâwin—an episode
that is most incongruous and *bizarre*. There is
another special criticism to be made. In nearly every book that he has written the author is
very free with casual allusions to persons and
things that presuppose a knowledge on the
reader's part of all his other books; but in
Mike Fletcher he refers to incidents which even
to one who remembers every line that he
has written are wholly unintelligible; so that
more than once a particularly exasperating
vagueness settles down upon the mind to be-
fog the interest and destroy the continuity of
the story.

Esther Waters was the first novel of Mr.
Moore's to be reprinted in the United States,
and it is still the only one by which in this
country he is generally known. It is inferior
to *A Mummer's Wife*, and, as a whole, to *A
Modern Lover* and *Mike Fletcher;* but the first
half of it contains some of the very best of all

its author's work. It tells the story of an English servant-maid, and it is written as a human document illustrative of the life, the ethics, and the average experiences of the class to which Esther herself belongs. Esther Waters goes out to service in the family of a country gentleman; she is betrayed by one of the grooms, is turned out of her place, and is thrown upon her own resources. The portions of the book which tell of her life immediately before the birth of her child, of her hospital experiences, and of the struggle for a livelihood that follows, are very powerfully written. Mr. Moore succeeds here, as he has nowhere else so perfectly succeeded, in touching the sources of sympathy and of pity. One reads these pages with an emotion that is almost irresistible, and that is the very strongest tribute to their author's grasp on life. But after that point in the story is reached where Esther's groom returns and marries her, and they settle down to the keeping of a "pub," and, on the husband's part, to the experiences of a typical British book-maker, the intensity of the interest wanes rapidly. The novel then becomes too obviously a *Tendenzroman*, after the fashion of Zola's *L'Argent*, and is in its too apparent purpose almost a tract against the universal

British vice of betting. The low life which Mr.
Moore here depicts is given with extraordinary accuracy of detail, and the picture is of
much sociological interest, but it is always
borne in upon the reader that the facts have
been "got up" for the occasion, and, unlike M.
Zola in his similar performances, Mr. Moore
has not the heat and glow of a great creative
imagination to fuse his raw material into a
dramatically satisfying whole.

A book of his called *Celibates*, which appeared in 1895, contains three stories, two of them
very short and comparatively unimportant,
though striking and original; but the third,
which is almost long enough to be called a
novel, is a very memorable piece of work. I
think it not only the most remarkable thing
that Mr. Moore has ever done, but as a piece
of minute observation and psychological analysis, one of the most extraordinary things in all
modern literature. It is entitled *Mildred Lawson*, and, summarized briefly, is the story of a
young Englishwoman reared among commonplace and comfortable surroundings, but filled
with a belief that life has some higher mission
for her than house-keeping and the bearing
of children. Having some money of her own,
she takes up painting, studies in London, hires

an apartment in Paris, becomes a Bohemian of
the extreme type, and flits about in a society
that is frankly beyond the pale of decency.
Yet because of her own coldness of temperament and her perpetual thought of self, she
remains physically pure, and we leave her toss-
ing about upon her bed with the cry, "Give
me a passion for God or man, but give me a
passion! I cannot live without one!"

There is probably no living writer in any
language who could have drawn this curiously subtle character as Mr. Moore has drawn it,
with a feeling for the most evanescent *nuances*
of temperament and a knowledge of certain
phases and types that is absolutely marvellous. This story, in fact, should properly rank
its author with the greatest masters of fiction
—with Stendhal and Balzac and Flaubert and
Thackeray; yet it will not do so, and for a very
obvious reason. When one thinks of it, why
does it happen that the epoch-making novelists just named have not only won an enduring
artistic success, but what may be called a popular success as well, so that their names and
their works alike are familiar to all cultivated
men and women? It is not merely because of
their genius and their profound knowledge of
life, their subtlety and the perfection of their

literary methods. It is first of all because they
have exercised these gifts and qualities in a field
that is familiar to all who read. The types
they draw are, in general, the types that the
most casual person can recognize and judge.
Every man of the world has, in his own experience, met Major Pendennis and Costigan
and Colonel Newcome. Becky Sharp has flit-
ted across the life of every one who lives in
the greater world. The tragedy of Père Go-
riot is enacted daily before the eyes of all of
us. Every provincial town contains an Emma
Bovary. Therefore, when these and others of
their general ubiquity appear in the pages of
a master, the perfect truth of the portraiture
is at once perceived by all, and the achievement is hailed with universal pleasure and applause. But in drawing Mildred Lawson, Mr.
Moore has deliberately fixed upon a type which
is not a common one as yet, though it will
grow commoner, I think, as society develops
on its present lines. It is a type that even
men of wide experience may not have happened to encounter; and so, in reading this
most subtle study, they may view it as a pure
invention of the novelist, wonderfully consistent and impressive to be sure, but one that
does not quite belong to actual life. They will

style it an abstraction, a mere personification
of certain intellectual and moral qualities, the
work of a literary Frankenstein, curious and
masterly, but on the whole unreal. And this
is the penalty which Mr. Moore must pay for
his daring and for his devotion to what he feels
to be the truth; for the type does actually exist, and with those who know it, its complexity
and its psychological abnormality, which partly
elude and partly appall the analyst, can only
heighten the unqualified amazement that is
the one appropriate tribute to Mr. Moore's almost incredible success.

The rarity of the type drawn in Mildred
Lawson is due to the fact that she combines so
many different qualities, as to become a com-
plex and not even a fairly simple character.
One sees in these days many women who are
at war with their environment and galled by
conventionality, who have educated themselves
beyond the control of every-day principles of
conduct, and who are bent upon " living their
own life," as the slang of the hour describes it.
One sees many women, also, of great cleverness and imagination and subtlety; and of
course one meets women of beauty and fascination and refinement. Nor is there any
dearth of women who are introspective and

self-analytical to the point of morbidity, and who in consequence are selfish in the intellectual as well as in the moral sense of that comprehensive word. But what one very seldom sees is a woman who combines all of these qualities and attributes—who is beautiful, accomplished, and fascinating, imaginative and intellectual, absolutely unfettered by the traditional limitations that have their root in centuries of social conventions, and yet so self-centred and acutely conscious of self as to find in this one trait the check upon conduct as well as upon achievement which in others of her sex arises from the thought of extraneous opinion. Now Mildred Lawson is the embodiment of all these characteristics; and to one who knows her type in life, the study that Mr. Moore has given of her is, down to its very last and subtlest tint, a masterpiece.

At the time when his book first appeared I said, in writing of the character of Mildred Lawson, that it suggests a blend of Becky Sharp and Blanche Amory; but such a generalization is altogether crude and superficial. Beside Mildred Lawson, Becky Sharp is commonplace, and Blanche Amory is a bit of rather vulgar affectation. Mildred Lawson's dominant traits are curiosity and imagination. She

wishes to know every phase of life, to experience everything, to feel every passion, every
emotion. Her imaginative mind shows her in
anticipation wonderful things — the pleasure
that comes from novelty, from achievement,
from love, from passion. She figures it all to
herself beforehand and thrills at the promise
of it all. But the very intensity of the anticipation makes the reality when it approaches
seem poor; it is, after all, not what she hoped
for, and she draws back from it with a kind
of shrinking distaste. She has divined what
ought to be the emotion for each phase of experience, and at the critical moment she falls
to analyzing the emotion until it vanishes and
she is disillusioned. It is the cult of self, and
it brings with it a fatal slavery. Even when
tragedy enters into her immediate life she
cannot suffer; she can only wonder why she
does not feel what she knows she ought to
feel. There is a conflict of thought and motive at every moment. A young artist who
had loved her, and for whom she had felt a
sort of patronizing fondness, sends for her as
he is dying:

"A close observer might have noticed that the expression on Mildred's face changed a little. 'He is
dying for me,' she thought. And, as in a ray of sun-

light, she basked for a moment in a little glow of self-
satisfaction.   Then almost angrily she defended herself against herself.   She was not responsible for so
casual a thought; the greatest saint might be a victim
of a wandering thought.   She was, of course, glad that
he liked her, but she was sorry that she caused him
suffering.   He must have suffered.   Men will sacrifice
anything to their passions. . . . They had had very
pleasant times together — in this very gallery. . . .
Suddenly her thoughts became clear and she heard
these words as if they had been read to her: ' Lots of
men have killed themselves for women, but to die of
a broken heart proves a great deal more.   Few women
have inspired such a love as that.' "

When her own brother dies she is overcome
with a desire to weep, but she first carefully
takes off her gown lest she should spoil it in
abandoning herself to grief.   Then she wonders
whether that was really her reason, after all.
Her love affairs were quite as fully mingled
with doubts and shrinkings and hesitations.
She has no principle ; the question of morality
does not enter her mind.   She is longing for
the thrill of passion.   It will be a new experience.   She is ready for it.   So at Barbizon,
where she goes to paint, she meets in that
beautiful spot, amid the scent of flowers and
the dewy dusk of the great forest, an English
painter—a frank sensualist, a man of physical

charm and with the added attractions of talent
and fame. They roam the forest together. She
thinks of how she longs for him. She would like
to take him in her arms and kiss him. When
they reach the very heart of the dim forest,
with its endless billows of dark-green foliage
and its mysterious murmurings instinct with
nature, she wonders whether he will kiss
her, whether he will take her hand and tell
her how he loves her. But he does not understand her, though he partly divines her
thought. Her curious uncertainty, that stifles
desire at the very moment when promise approaches fulfilment, makes her manner half-
repellent. Yet the two go on together with a
curious frankness. They discuss Morton's former mistresses; they stick at nothing in word
and phrase—but Mildred still shrinks from the
critical step. She cannot feel the self-abandonment, the sublime unconsciousness that marks
the triumph of love. And so the story is un-
folded. She longs to do something really
great, but her talent is not adequate for that,
and she cares for nothing that is less than
great. She longs for love, but her heart is
cold and her emotions dulled. She fascinates
others; she is brilliant, good-natured in a way,
with that careless good-nature which is often

the very refinement of cruelty in that it is at bottom quite indifferent ; and she dissects and vivisects herself at every turn until she gets at last a horrible understanding of her own real nature.

"Self had been her ruin ; she had never been able to get away from self ; no, not for a single moment of her life. All her love-stories had been ruined and disfigured by self-assertion—not a great, unconscious self, in other words, an instinct, but an extremely conscious, irritable, mean, and unworthy self. She knew it all ; she was not deceived. She could no more cheat herself than she could change herself ; that wretched self was as present in her at this moment as it had ever been, and knowledge of her fault helped her nothing in its correction. She could not change herself ; she would have to bear the burden of herself to the end."

The picture is astonishing ; and one despairs in attempting to convey to those who have not read the book even a faint conception of the startling power of analysis which it everywhere displays.

It has been said above that Mr. Moore has given to English literature an entirely new *genre*, and this is true ; for though, after he returned to England, he won back his English style, he has never separated himself from the

French school of literary art in which he received his earliest training; and he is to-day to
be grouped, not with Hardy and Hope and
Besant, but with far greater artists than even
the first of these—with **Guy de Maupassant**
and Zola and J. K. Huysmans. He is, in fact,
the only writer of English who exemplifies the
whole manner and spirit of the Realists. In
everything but his language he is French, and
not only French but Parisian. His models,
his standards, his whole technique he finds
among the writers of France; and one is not
surprised on learning that it was he who first
made known to the English the works of Verlaine and Rimbaud and Jules Laforge. There
is not a single one of his longer novels that
is not demonstrably inspired or sensibly influenced by some great French masterpiece.
The seduction of Kate Lennox, in *A Mummer's Wife*, and her gradual degradation
through drink, must be regarded as a reminis-
cence of the story of Gervaise in *L'Assommoir*.
Mike Fletcher, who takes money from women
and rises by their favor from back-alley journal-
ism to fortune, is only an English (or Irish)
replica of Georges Duroy in *Bel-Ami*. The
story of *Esther Waters* is an evident borrowing
from the Goncourts' *Germinie Lacerteux*, with

a greater minuteness of obstetrical description. In fact, while Mr. Moore is not a copyist, he is so saturated with the theories of the Realistic School as to make it impossible for him to avoid the reproduction of their themes.

Nor is it merely in his themes that he recalls his Gallic masters. The pessimism of his writings makes him still more closely kin to them ; and for this his Celtic origin is undoubtedly responsible, since the pessimism of the Celt is something to which the Anglo-Saxon can never by any possibility attain. The Celt, whether he be Irish or French, is always a creature of extremes. Light-hearted with a delightful joyousness and frivolity, he is, in his other mood, hopeless with an abysmal misery. The Anglo-Saxon, on the other hand, though he takes his pleasure sadly, takes his sorrow hopefully, and has an element of sturdy resistance in his nature that defies destiny and smites the inevitable in the face. The gloom of the Anglo-Saxon is a melancholy half-light ; the gloom of the Celt is the blackness that presses on the eye-balls like a physical weight, and plunges the very soul into infinite despair. Mr. Hardy, for instance, gives us a fine expression of Anglo-Saxon pessimism. Things are often ordered for the very worst in this world ; but he accepts

the worst, and can still perceive the humor that
forever gleams amid the irony of fate. But the
pessimism of a Maupassant is a grim, intense,
and all-including monotony of horror that
taints and corrodes like a mordant acid. And
so nothing in all literature is more hideous
than the last twenty pages of *Mike Fletcher*,
after reading which one feels for the moment
that life itself is a loathsome thing, pregnant
with shame and nameless evil.

How purely French is Mr. Moore's literary
method can perhaps best be seen in what he
has written as a critic of literature and art.
To the general reading public his most important book of criticism is the one which in form
is nearest akin to the conventional volume of
essays, such as American and English writers
put forth from time to time. Yet it is not
in *Impressions and Opinions* that one finds the
true George Moore, but in a curious and fascinating little volume entitled *The Confessions
of a Young Man*, put forth several years ago,
and reprinted in this country, where it slowly
passed into a second edition. This book, which
is unique in English literature, is nominally the
autobiography of one Edward Dayne; but it
may very fairly be regarded as containing a
suggestion, and something more than a suggest-

ion, of the facts of Mr. Moore's own personal
history. The thread of story, however, is a
very slight one, and is broken and intercalated with disconnected and apparently irrelevant
paragraphs that touch upon the most diverse
questions of art, literature, and morals. Thus,
à propos of nothing in particular, the author
will drop the narrative of Dayne's financial
troubles, or of his *vie de Bohème*, to express a
terse judgment on the Symbolists, or on the
impossibility of marriage among enlightened
persons, or on the artistic value of the music-
hall, or on the respective merits of the eigh-
teenth-century tavern and the nineteenth-cen-
tury club; or he will pause to discourse with
curious psychological subtlety on *la femme de
trente ans*, and then suddenly slip back into
the narration that he has temporarily put
aside. The lack of form in all this is, to a
conventionally Anglo-Saxon reader, exasperating and eccentric; to others it is simply piquant; but in reality it is part of a perfectly
consistent design in that it gives us a picture
of mentality, of an intellectual and æsthetic
condition, and thus fits in perfectly with the
synchronous picture of a human life. In this,
moreover, Mr. Moore is not violating literary
precedent—he is following it; only the model

that he has before him is French, not English.
It is as old as Jean Paul; it is as new as Maurice Barrès; and, in fact, it is probably the
curious *Ennemi des Lois* of Barrès that Mr.
Moore is consciously imitating in his plan, although he does not specifically mention that
odd and brilliant writer. And the opinions
themselves are strikingly original—audacious,
independent, perverse, absolutely un-English,
wholly French. Take this, for example:

"I am sick of synthetical art; we want observation
direct and unreasoned. What I reproach Millet with
is that it is always the same thing, the same peasant,
the same *sabot*, the same sentiment. You must admit
that it is somewhat stereotyped. What does this matter? What is more stereotyped than Japanese art?
But that does not prevent it from being always beautiful."

This is thinking aloud. Then take the following:

"How to be happy!—not to read Baudelaire and
Verlaine, not to enter the 'Nouvelle Athènes,' unless
perhaps to play dominos like the *bourgeois* over
there, not to do anything that would awake a too intense consciousness of life—to live in a sleepy country-side, to have a garden to work in, to have a wife
and children, to chatter quietly every evening over
the details of existence. We must have the azaleas

8

out to-morrow and thoroughly cleansed, they are devoured by insects; the tame rook has flown away; mother lost her prayer-book coming from church; she thinks it was stolen. A good, honest, well-to-do peasant, who knows nothing of politics, must be very nearly happy—and to think there are people who would educate, who would draw these people out of the calm satisfaction of their instincts and give them passions. The philanthropist is the Nero of modern times."

Here is a bit of personal feeling that is as French as though written by a Frenchman:

"The years the most impressionable, from twenty to thirty, when the senses and the mind are the widest awake, I, the most impressionable of human beings, had spent in France, not among English residents, but among that which is the quintessence of the nation; I, not an indifferent spectator, but an enthusiast, striving heart and soul to identify himself with his environment, to shake himself free from race and language, and to recreate himself, as it were, in the womb of a new nationality, assuming its ideals, its morals, and its modes of thought; and I had succeeded strangely well, and when I returned home England was a new country to me; I had, as it were, forgotten everything. Every aspect of street and suburban garden was new to me; of the manner of life of Londoners I knew nothing. This sounds incredible; but it is so. I saw, but I could realize nothing. I went into a drawing-room, but everything seemed far away—a dream, a presentment, nothing more; I was in touch

with nothing; of the thoughts and feelings of those I
met I could understand nothing, nor could I sympa-
thize with them; an Englishman was at that time as
much out of my mental reach as an Esquimau would
be now. Women were nearer to me than men, and I
will take this opportunity to note my observation, for
I am not aware that any one else has observed that
the difference between the two races is found in the
men, not in the women. French and English women
are psychologically very similar; the standpoint from
which they see life is the same, the same thoughts interest and amuse them; but the attitude of a Frenchman's mind is absolutely opposed to that of an Englishman; they stand on either side of a vast abyss,
two animals different in color, form, and temperament—two ideas destined to remain irrevocably sep-
arate and distinct."

Mr. Moore has something to say of contemporary English literature. Here are some
rather curious bits. The first has to do with
Mr. Robert Louis Stevenson.

"I will state frankly that Mr. R. L. Stevenson never
wrote a line that failed to delight me; but he never
wrote a book. . . . I think of Mr. Stevenson as a con-
sumptive youth weaving garlands of sad flowers with
pale, weak hands, or leaning to a large plate-glass
window and scratching thereon exquisite profiles with
a diamond pencil. . . . I do not care to speak of great
ideas, for I am unable to see how an idea can exist,
at all events can be great, out of language; an allusion to Mr. Stevenson's verbal expression will perhaps

make my meaning clear.   His periods are fresh and
bright, rhythmical in sound, and perfect realizations
of their sense; in reading you often think that never
before was such definiteness united to such poetry of
expression; every page and every sentence rings of
its individuality. Mr. Stevenson's style is over-smart—
well dressed, shall I say?—like a young man walking
in the Burlington Arcade.   Yes, I will say so; but, I
will add, the most gentlemanly young man that ever
walked on the Burlington.   Mr. Stevenson is competent to understand any thought that might be presented to him; but if he were to use it, it would instantly become neat, sharp, ornamental, light, and
graceful; and it would lose all its original richness
and harmony.   It is not Mr. Stevenson's brain that
prevents him from being a thinker, but his style."

And this is what he has to say of Mr. George
Meredith :

" ' When we have translated half of Mr. Meredith's
utterances into possible human speech, then we can
enjoy him,' says the *Pall Mall Gazette*.   We take our
pleasures differently ; mine are spontaneous, and I
know nothing about translating the rank smell of a
nettle into the fragrance of a rose, and than enjoy-
ing it.

" Mr. Meredith's conception of life is crooked, ill-
balanced, and out of tune.   What remains ?   A certain lustiness.   You have seen a big man with square
shoulders and a small head pushing about in a crowd;
he shouts and works his arms; he seems to be doing
a great deal; in reality, he is doing nothing.   So Mr.

Meredith appears to me, and yet I can only think of
him as an artist. His habit is not slatternly, like those
of such literary hodmen as Mr. David Christie Mur-
ray, Mr. Besant, Mr. Buchanan. There is no trace of
the crowd about him. I do not question his right of
place. I am out of sympathy with him—that is all ;
and I regret that it should be so, for he is one whose
love of art is pure and untainted with commercialism ;
and if I may praise it for naught else, I can praise it
for this."

What he says of Mr. Hardy is particularly
interesting, for it shows what I have always
said, that, with all Mr. Hardy's pessimism and
with all his frankness on certain social questions, he is still essentially Anglo-Saxon, and
is therefore, from the French point of view,
likely to be misjudged and misunderstood.

" His work is what dramatic critics would call good,
honest, straightforward work. It is unillumined by
a ray of genius ; it is slow and somewhat sodden. It
reminds me of an excellent family coach—one of the
old sort—hung on C-springs, a fat coachman on the
box, and a footman whose livery was made for his
predecessor. In criticising Mr. Meredith I was out of
sympathy with my author, ill at ease, angry, puzzled ;
but with Mr. Hardy I am on quite different terms. I
am as familiar with him as with the old pair of trousers I put on when I sit down to write. I know all
about his aims, his methods. I know what has been
done in that line, and what can be done."

The following dictum is not wholly, perhaps, unfair to Mr. Henry James, but it is decidedly unjust to Mr. Howells:

"What Mr. James wants to do is what he does. I will admit that an artist may be great and limited ; by one word he may light up an abyss of soul ; but there must be this one magical and unique word. Shakespeare gives us the word ; Balzac sometimes, after pages of vain striving, gives us the word ; Tourguénieff gives it with miraculous certainty ; but Henry James, no. A hundred times he flutters about it ; his whole book is one long flutter near to the one magical and unique word, but the word is not spoken ; and for want of the word his characters are never resolved out of the haze or nebulæ. You are on a bowing acquaintance with them. They pass you in the street, they stop and speak to you ; you know how they are dressed ; you watch the color of their eyes. . . . I have seen a good many people I knew. I have observed an attitude and an earnestness of manner that proved that a heart was beating. . . . I have read nothing of Henry James's that did not suggest the manner of a scholar. But why should a scholar limit himself to empty and endless sentimentalities ? I will not taunt him with any of the old taunts. Why does he not write complicated stories ? Why does he not complete his stories ? Let all this be waived. I will ask him only why he always avoids decisive action ? Why does a woman never say 'I will' ? Why does a woman never leave the house with her lover ? Why does a man never kill a man ? Why does a man never kill

himself? Why is nothing ever accomplished? In
real life, murder, adultery, and suicide are of common occurrence; but Mr. James's people live in a
calm, sad, and very polite twilight volition. Suicide
or adultery has happened before the story begins;
suicide or adultery happens some years hence, when
the characters have left the stage; but bang in front of
the reader nothing happens. . . . In connection with
Henry James I had often heard the name of W. D.
Howells. I bought some three or four of his novels.
I found them pretty, very pretty, but nothing more—
a sort of Ashby Sterry done into very neat prose. He
is vulgar, is refined as Henry James; he is more domestic; girls with white dresses and virginal looks,
languid mammas, mild witticisms, here, there, and
everywhere; a couple of young men, one a little cynical, the other a little overshadowed by his love; a
strong, bearded man of fifty in the background; in a
word, a Tom Robertson comedy faintly spiced with
American. Henry James went to France and read
Tourguénieff. W. D. Howells stayed at home and
read Henry James."

It is impossible to sum up Mr. Moore as a
critic in any very satisfactory way. He is
frankly a decadent, frankly a sensualist, but
a decadent and a sensualist of the type of
Huysmans, whom he intensely admires:

"A page of Huysmans is as a dose of opium, a
glass of some exquisite and powerful liqueur. . . .
Huysmans goes to my soul like a gold ornament of

Byzantine workmanship. There is in his style the yearning charm of arches, a sense of ritual, the passion of the mural, of the window."

But Mr. Moore's affinity with Huysmans does not go further than a certain sensuous sympathy. He could never follow him in that curious transformation of which I have elsewhere written, because he has never followed him to the full in the unrelieved brutality that was the essential condition of an ultimate reaction. Mr. Moore must remain intellectually apart from any actual translation of thought into action; he must go on stirred by strange thoughts, forever sensitive to the subtlest æsthetic influences, but to the very last resisting absolutely any impulse towards a definite and final *rangement*.

A word must be said of his style and literary expression; and here again the same analogies with the French are unmistakable. As his critical writing recalls the manner of Barrès and his associates, so his fiction is in style most powerfully dominated by the influence of Zola. This likeness is, indeed, the very first that strikes the casual reader of his pages. He is Zolaesque in his keen perception of the purely physical side of every scene, of every episode, and even of those situations that are properly and primarily psychological. Like Zola, he tries to see a sort of harmony between a state of mind and its external setting. Like Zola, too, and the other naturalistic writers, his sense of smell is exceedingly acute, and his odor-scheme is as well defined as is the color-scheme of Mr. Stephen Crane, and far less fanciful. He never spares you even the most nauseous osmic detail of the sick-room, of the slum, of the stale and stifling boozing-ken. In his ballroom scenes, under the fragrance of crushed and dying flowers and the most exquisite perfumes, he will detect and note the scent of perspiration, the suggestion of bared necks and arms. The escaping gas of the theatre, the whiff from the sewer-opening, and the indescribable sourness of the drunkard, all run through his descriptive passages like a musical accompaniment—a *motif* directed through the nostrils to the mind. This is reminiscent of Zola, and of Maupassant, the great high-priest of the sense of smell; but it is not imitative, for it is just as natural to Mr. Moore as it is to these great writers, and it is wonderfully effective in its psychical results. We get in him, for example, not merely the Paris that meets the casual eye, but the Paris that is perceptible to the nose as well—the *bouquet* of the boulevard,

the blend of leaves and earth, of wet as-
phalt, of flaring gas and of cookery, suffused
with the suggestion of wine and cigarette
smoke, and just a whiff of opoponax and cory-
lopsis from the perfumed silks and laces that
brush against us in the gliding throng.   To
read some paragraphs of *Celibates* gives the
exiled *flâneur* a curious reminiscent thrill that
almost pulses into pain.   Yet, though these
subtle appeals to a sense too greatly scorned
by the Anglo-Saxon are oftenest made through
media that offend, it is only fair to say that,
like Zola, and in a far higher degree, Mr.
Moore is acutely sensitive to what is beautiful in nature.   Some of his descriptions,
though nearly always brief, are exquisitely
realized, and are set in language that en-
chants the ear, and through the ear the imagination.   Take this of the forest at Barbizon :

"There was an opening in the trees, and below that
the dark-green forest waved for miles.   It was pleasant to rest—they were tired.   The forest murmured
like a shell. . . . It extended like a great temple, hush-
ed in the ritual of the sunset.   The light that suffused
the green leaves overhead glossed the brown leaves
underfoot, marking the smooth ground as with a
pattern.   And like chapels every dell seemed in the
tranquil light, and leading from them a labyrinthine

architecture without design or end. Mildred's eyes
wandered from the colonnades to the underwoods.
She thought of the forest as of a great green prison;
and then her soul fled to the scraps of blue that appeared through the thick leafage, and she longed for
large spaces of sky, for a view of a plain, for a pine-
plumed hill-top."

"The forest murmured like a shell." That
is one of the most exquisite touches of description that the English language owns; and the
whole passage gives, as no painted picture,
whether of Cazin or of Harpignies, can ever
give, the full effect upon the senses of a vast
forest, of its immensity, of its beauty, and of
its overpowering oppressiveness.

Here is Kate Lennox, as we first meet her,
in *A Mummer's Wife*:

"Nothing was now heard but the methodical click
of her needle as it struck the head of her thimble, and
then the long swish of the thread as she drew it
through the cloth. The lamp at her elbow burned
steadily, and the glare glanced along her arm as she
raised it with the large movement of sewing. Wherever the light touched it her hair was blue, and it en-
circled, like a piece of rich black velvet, the white but
too prominent temples; a dark shadow defined the
fine, straight nose, hinted at a thin indecision of lips,
whilst a broad touch of white marked the weak but
not unbeautiful chin. On her knees lay the patch-

work, with its jagged edges, and the floor at her feet was covered with innumerable scraps, making a red and black litter."

Few Anglo-Saxons ever fully entertain a true conception of word-values as the French do, and as George Moore has done. That the exact word always exists, and that any word but the exact word breaks the connection between the writer and the reader's minds, is a fact of which few English or Americans in these slipshod days are cognizant; but with George Moore, half sensitivist and half sensualist, and fed on Mallarmé and Hérédia, the cult of *le mot juste* is a passion. What can be more perfect as an example of cadenced melody than what he has written of Gustave Kahn's *Intermède* ?

"The repetitions of Edgar Poe seem hard and mechanical after this, so exquisite and evanescent is the rhythm, and the intonations come as sweetly and suddenly as a gust of perfume; it is as the vibration of a fairy orchestra, flute and violin disappearing in a silver mist; but the clouds break, and all the enchantment of a spring garden appears in a shaft of sudden sunlight."

Our English tongue can get no nearer than it has done here to supreme felicity of phrasing.

As a bit of striking personal description and

as the last of these quotations, I select Moore's interesting account of his first meeting with Paul Verlaine, recorded in *Impressions and Opinions :*

"We got into an omnibus, and then we got into a tram. Then we took a cab, and I believe we had to take another tram. We passed factories and canals, and at one moment I thought we were going to take the boat. We at last penetrated into a dim and eccentric region which I had never heard of before. We traversed curious streets, inhabited apparently by people who in dressing never got further than *camisoles* and shirt sleeves ; we penetrated into musty-smelling and clamorous court-yards, in which lingered Balzacian *concierges ;* we climbed slippery staircases upon which doors stood wide open, emitting odors and permitting occasional views of domestic life—a man in his shirt hammering a boot, a woman, presumably a mother, wiping a baby. . . . In a dark corner, at the end of a narrow passage situated at the top of the last flight of stairs, we discovered a door. We knocked. A voice made itself heard. We entered and saw Verlaine. The terrible forehead, bald and prominent, was half covered by a filthy nightcap, and a night-shirt full of the grease of the bed covered his shoulders ; a stained and discolored pair of trousers were hitched up somehow about his waist. He was drinking wine at sixteen sous the litre. He told us that he had just come out of the hospital ; that his leg was better, but it still gave him a great deal of pain. He pointed to it. We looked away.

" He said he was writing the sonnet, and promised
that we should have it on the morrow. Then, in the
grossest language, he told us of the abominations he
had included in the sonnet ; and seeing that our visit
would prove neither pleasant nor profitable, we took
our leave as soon as we could."

It remains only to consider what appears
to be the most serious and constantly recurring limitation upon Mr. Moore's extraordinary
power as a delineator of contemporary life and
manners. With all his acuteness of observation, with all his sureness of touch, with all his
insight and experience, it is impossible to over-
look the very important fact that this insight
and experience are very closely circumscribed
by what one can only call his ignorance of the
brighter side of the social world. Mr. Moore's
social attitude is that of a man who has lived
in clubs and mingled with men of the world
only in those hours which they give to what is
usually known as pleasure. His views are the
sort of views that one may always hear set
forth in the club smoking-room, and his
notion of domestic life is the notion formed
by one who takes all this cynicism literally
and as representing a permanent and predom-
inant state of mind. But every one of large
experience knows how utterly misleading all

this is, especially when noted among men of our own race. That the cynic of the smoking-room will, over his *petit verre* and a good cigar, tell improper little stories of the world in which he lives, that he gibes at marriage, that he professes to suspect the virtue of all women, that he airs theories which are at variance with all the traditions of his people—this means absolutely less than nothing in a vast majority of instances. It is the idle talk of men who are in reality tender-hearted, loyal, devoted, reverent, and true; and when any one, like Mr. Moore, constructs for himself a society upon the basis of these post-cenatory conversations he is mistaking an idle phase for a permanent condition. Now the social world that one discovers in Mr. Moore's novels is essentially a mirage of the clubs, and not a thing of which he has a first-hand knowledge. A very brilliant woman of my acquaintance, and one whose invincible determination not to write inflicts a real loss on English literature, has expressed this thought in a figurative sort of way. " It is a pity," she said, after reading one of his novels, " that George Moore is not sometimes willing to drink a cup of tea in the afternoon." But he never is; and brandy-and-soda is about the only beverage suggested by his writing.

This would be no defect at all if he were strictly to confine himself to the actual corner of the world which he knows so well. The innermost recesses of Bohemia, the sweltering slum, the race-course, the public-house, the shop, the *atelier*, the club—here he is quite supreme, a master of detail, a rhyparographer as faithful as Eumachus or the Flemish painters. But he is not content with this. In *A Modern Lover* and *A Drama in Muslin* and *Mike Fletcher* he tries to lead us elsewhere and to show us the English home, the country-side, the men and women who live far from Curzon Street and who know not Leicester Square or the " Empire." And then he fails, and fails in a way that not only disappoints but utterly repels; for here in the quiet nooks and in an atmosphere of tranquillity and peace he shows us still the rakes and bullies, the immodest women, the intrigue, and the assignation. The fragrance of the hedgerows is tainted by patchouly and by chypre; and the heavy opium-charged scent of the Egyptian cigarette comes to our nostrils in the quiet country lanes. To read some of these pages is like witnessing the *danse du ventre* performed around a May-pole. It is false; it is monstrous; it is actually loathsome.

The club smoking-room is suggested also by the language in which Mr. Moore has set down much of what he writes. One does not mind his coarseness merely because it is coarse, but because of its frequent inappropriateness, because he is himself quite conscious of his offence, and because it is tainted by an almost omnipresent suggestion of vulgarity. He has some compunction himself on this score, but he drugs his literary conscience with the quite untenable belief that he is representing a genuine reversion to the freer speech of Fielding and of Smollett; whereas Fielding and Smollett, while often coarse, were never vulgar. They used the language and the phrases of their day with simplicity and complete unconsciousness; while Mr. Moore, with other standards and in a modern age, is forcing a note, and a very false one, in his effort to produce what at its best is but a pure anachronism.

But this defect of his goes even deeper down; and one must frankly say that the source of his vulgarity is more than superficial and comes from something more than a mistaken choice of models. It is far more fundamental, for it colors his whole view of human life and makes this in its last analysis the life of swine and apes. His revelry is not the care-

9

less revelry of youth, soon set aside for the
soberer duties of maturity ; it is studied sen-
sualism reduced to a science whose joyless-
ness is as striking as its depravity.   It has no
mirth, no spontaneity; its record gives us only
the impression of jaded senses frantically seeking some new stimulant, loud, mirthless laugh-
ter, and the sodden discontent that sits amid
the stale odors of the feast in the gray hours
of the morning, when the bloodshot eye and
the twitching face look spectral in the ghastly
light of dawn.

And the persons whom he draws for us are
fit for such a life as he describes.   His women
are of two set types.   One is the bold-eyed, full-
lipped woman whose person exhales a subtle
suggestion of sensuality, and who is ever seeking a seducer.   From the young girl in the con-
vent - school to the matron in the ball-room,
this is the type that Mr. Moore again and
again is meeting and describing with a strange
power of erotic suggestion, and a thorough disbelief in the endurance of virtue for any longer
time than that required to furnish an opportunity for sin.   Chastity, when he does discover it, is not a matter of conscience, but is
purely temperamental.   A woman may be
chaste just as she may be cross-eyed.   She is

not responsible for either. Some natures are too cold to sin; they shrink from it only because its promise does not stir them; and in his philosophy natures such as these are rare and utterly abnormal. But over them George Moore devotes little time and thought. He sets the other type before us with a never-ending and persistent relish. When there appears upon the scene a woman's form, he thrusts it on us like a professional *souteneur*. With a frank brutality he catalogues her physical attractions; a pervasive suggestion inspires his pen; he mentally disrobes her, and he laughs softly with the cynical amusement of a Silenus as he notes the effect of his description.

His men are, naturally enough, the moral complement of his women. He has never drawn one noble character, and there is no evidence in any of his work that he even comprehends the English and American conception of a high-bred gentleman. His world is a world of rakes and revellers, of cads, of 'Arries and 'Arriets, with here and there a solitary figure, eccentric and unmanly, whose thin blood or mediæval imagination leads him to slink into pure asceticism and to shudder at the joys of sense. And as among his women we miss the unselfish, the tender, the loyal, and

the loving, so among his men we find no high-
minded, generous, manly gentleman whose chivalry and purity of soul remove him to an equal
distance from the monkey-cage and the mon-
astic cell.

Such, then, is George Moore—a strange and
striking product of French training, a blend of
subtlety and coarseness, of cynicism and vo-
luptuousness, of extreme refinement and inef-
fable vulgarity; a profound psychologist, a
sensitivist who feels to his very finger-tips the
slightest breath of influence, a genius fettered
by the chains of pure materialism, yet none
the less and with all his limitations and perversities the greatest literary artist who has
struck the chords of English since the death
of Thackeray.

THE EVOLUTION OF A MYSTIC

THE EVOLUTION OF A MYSTIC

WHAT is the psychological secret of the mysterious connection that exists between religious desire in man and the desire that is sensuous and even sensual? That there is some such relation it is impossible to doubt when we look into the records alike of literature and of life. Let one turn to the confessions of Saint Augustine, the loftiest and greatest of the Latin Fathers, and read the appalling chronicle of those wallowings in sin through which he ultimately passed to the saintly life that still shines with undimmed purity down the path of human effort. Let one also call to mind the strangely dual life of Paul Verlaine, who so often sat down, recking with the odors of the foulest of Parisian *gargotes*, to pour out in verse of almost superhuman sweetness the aspirations of a soul profoundly touched with religious yearning. Nor is it without a deep significance that in ancient times the worship of the gods was

often blended with rites of indescribable eroti-
cism, and that in all ages the vocabulary of
religious exaltation has been borrowed from
the language of human passion. The Song
of Songs, ascribed to Solomon, is, to be sure,
no longer viewed as a sacred allegory; yet it
was for many centuries so regarded, and the
sternest and most ascetic Puritan was not re-
volted by the thought that its amorous imagery was meant to voice a spiritual sentiment. To take a very modern instance, it
was only a few years ago that one of the most
widely popular of evangelical hymns was criticised, and not quite unreasonably, because its
language was too emphatically suggestive of
mere sexual desire. It may be, in fact, that
there is something typical and significant in
the legend of Saint Anthony, one of the holiest of anchorites, whose chief temptation was
that which filled his cell with visions of fair
women.

The subject is, perhaps, a little dangerous,
and one need not here pursue it any further;
yet it is quite irresistibly suggested by a volume which now lies before me, entitled *En
Route*, and which one may without exaggeration think not only the greatest novel of the
day, but one of the most important, because

it is one of the most characteristic books of our quarter of the century. Until its author, M. Huysmans, wrote it, his name suggested to the readers of French literature nothing more than naturalistic fiction of the rankest and most brutal type—fiction that surpassed the most typical work of Zola in the frankness of its physiology and the shamelessness of its indecency. With *À Rebours*, which appeared in 1885, this Flemish Frenchman reached a sort of morbid climax both in subject and in treatment, and because of this Herr Nordau chose him out as embodying the quintessence of moral and literary degeneracy. Yet it seemed to many at the time of its appearance that in *À Rebours* there was to be detected a new and striking note, an indication of new currents of tendency, a drift away from merely physical analysis, a reaching out towards something which, if not ethically higher, was at any rate more subtle and more psychologically interesting. The later works of M. Huysmans have made it plain that this assumption was a true one ; and since *Là Bas* has been succeeded by this latest work, the true significance of the change is very clear. Taking these three novels together, one may rightly view them as embodying a single purpose — a purpose of which perhaps and probably the writer was himself not always fully conscious, but which, as his task proceeded, fully seized upon his intellect and was, no doubt, developed with the simultaneous development of his own experience.

For it is permissible to think that in setting before us the evolution of a true degenerate, M. Huysmans has been writing a spiritual and intellectual autobiography. Mr. Kegan Paul, to be sure, in an admirable introduction to his translation of the book, declares that such an assertion is both impertinent and unnecessary; but even he avoids a flat denial of its truth. Whether it be impertinent or not, it will occur with great force to every one who knows the story of M. Huysmans' life and who is thoroughly familiar with his works; nor can one think that the hypothesis is one which the author would himself resent. It seems, indeed, impossible that the strange things set forth in *À Rebours* could have been imagined by a person whose own life had been free from any such experience, or that the intensity of feeling that marks the strongest chapters of *En Route* could be merely the *tour de force* of a clever writer. We shall not, therefore, be far wrong if we assume that we have

now before us the record of a searching self-
analysis, however much the superficial incidents of the story be altered from the actual
facts. This must be borne in mind, for the
books, that form a sort of series, refer ostensi-
bly to different persons; yet it is, in reality,
but one single experience that M. Huysmans
is relating. For whether the protagonist be
spoken of as Des Esseintes in *À Rebours* or as
Durtal in *En Route*, the change of name implies no change in personality, nor in the conditions of the psychological and moral problem that is presented for our contemplation.

The story itself is the narrative of a man
who has deliberately cultivated sensation to
the point where it has touched the very extreme of enervation, and who in this persistent
quest has exhausted the possibilities of physical pleasure, until at last the morbid and the
abnormal have reached the narrow line that
marks the verge of sanity. This phase is set
before us in *À Rebours*, perhaps the strangest
effort of perverse imagination that literature
can show. Here we find the degenerate already sated with the pleasures of the flesh,
jaded and fatigued, yet seeking still for something to excite at least a momentary interest,
and endeavoring to find it in the piquancy

of a life in which everything shall be utterly
abnormal, in which all the modes and all the
conditions of ordinary existence shall be con-
sistently reversed.   He, therefore, creates for
himself a home apart from any possible contact with other men, where in every possible
way he follows out the cult of the artificial
as being the supreme attainment of human
genius.   He is served by unseen attendants,
who avoid entering his presence.   He never
quits his home.   He sleeps, when his insomnia
permits it, by day, and prowls about his habi-
tation in the hours when other men are sleeping.   His living-rooms are enclosed one within
another, with holes that admit an artificial
light through glass receptacles filled with water
colored by essences to a muddy yellow, and
containing mechanical fish that pass slowly
back and forth through clusters of sham sea-
weed.   The chamber is impregnated with the
smell of tar and decorated with crude litho-
graphs of ships and seascapes.   In this strange
place he amuses himself with experimenting
in the theories of Symbolism, translating each
of the senses into terms of another.   Wishing
to hear music, he summons its sensations by
drinking drops of curious liqueurs, whose effect
upon the taste excites in his mind the sensa-

tions analogous to those produced by different instruments of music—dry curaçoa recalling the clarinet, gin and whiskey the trombone, anisette the flute, and Chios-raki and mastic the cymbal and the kettledrum. When he longs for the effect produced by pictures, he obtains it through his sense of smell, mixing together the perfumes that bring up before his depraved imagination landscapes or city scenes, the dressing-room of the theatre, or the surgeon's clinic, where ulcers and festering wounds attract his thought. His morbid ingenuity evokes from every scent an optical sensation, from the smell of stephanotis and ayapana to that of ordure and of human sweat. When he eats, and before his body revolts from the abnormality of his tastes, he dines on buttered roast beef dipped in tea. There is no need to recapitulate the further details of this phase of his development. On the face of it there seems to be nothing in the tale but what is morbid and delirious, and to a healthy mind both hideous and revolting. Yet, as has been already said, one can here detect a subtle note that is not found in *Marthe* or *Sœurs Vatard*. The cult of the purely physical has ceased to satisfy, and there is a vaguely outlined longing for something intangible which the flesh alone cannot allay.

In *Là Bas*, the second novel of the series, this longing has taken a more definite form. We see a quite distinctly formulated interest in the spiritual, or at least the supernatural. Mere animalism retires into the background of the mental picture, though it still exists as a discordant and disturbing element. The degenerate hero of the book has turned his mind towards the phenomena of the religious sentiment as a sphere neglected heretofore, and perhaps quite capable of affording new sensations. Yet, as before in other things he utterly reversed all normal notions, so in this new quest his impulses are inspired by perversity. He approaches religion from the stand-point of its contemner. Where a normal sinner would seek the influence of prayer and worship, Durtal enrolls himself among those fearful creatures who embrace the cult of Satanism. These singular rites, as one tradition tells us, were brought to Western Europe from the East by the Knights Templars at the time of the Crusades, and were finally at least the pretext for the dissolution of that famous order. As many know, the cult survives in France, and has not been unknown in Eng-

land during the past hundred years; for students of literary history will remember how it
found a devotee in Lord le Despencer, who
practised it with men like Wilkes and Byron
and Paul Whitehead at Medmenham in the
old Cistercian abbey. Durtal is led by the
influence of one Madame Chantelouve, a dia-
bolic creature, to join in the frightful practices
of the Satanists. He is present at a Black
Mass, where blasphemy supplants the Litany,
where prayer is mocked by cursing, and where
images of the devil and his angels take the place
of God and of the saints. By Madame Chantelouve he is lured into various acts of sacrilege,
some of them involuntary; and thus he seems
to have sunk to an even lower depth than
when he lived the frankly pagan life of an eccentric decadent. Yet one feels in laying
down the book that the end is not yet; that
Durtal is still groping in the darkness, and
that the very violence and outrageousness of
his impulses may lead him at last into a reaction against the physical and moral disease
that vexes him.

In *En Route* we observe a striking contrast
at the very outset. Durtal is presented to us
as already weaned, in spirit at least, from the
life that he has led so long. He is shown as

one who has accepted in the fullest sense the faith of the Catholic Church. The processes of his conversion are not detailed, but they may be inferred from what is told us in the opening chapter. Led on by curiosity, and perhaps by a desire for new experiences, he began to study the manifestations of the religious sentiment, and at once his mind and imagination alike were seized and held fast by the artistic side of the Roman ritual. He set himself to learn the inner history of the Church, the lives of saints, and the story of passionate devotion which those lives have illustrated. He steeped himself in the spirit of the Middle Ages, and sought out those sanctuaries where that spirit still finds its manifestations apart from the sordidness of modern life. The stately Gregorian music, the child-like yet affecting forms of mediæval art, the ancient churches whose chapels are dimmed by the smoke of innumerable censers and impregnated with the odor of extinguished tapers and of burning incense, excited in him indescribable emotions.

"Among these [churches] St. Séverin seemed to Durtal the most exquisite and the most certain. He felt at home there ; he believed that if he could ever pray in earnest he could do it in that church ; and he said to himself that therein lived the spirit of the fabric. It is impossible but that the burning prayers, the hopeless sobs of the Middle Ages, have not forever impregnated the pillars and stained the walls; it is impossible but that the vine of sorrows whence of old the saints gathered warm clusters of tears has not preserved from those wonderful days emanations which sustain, a breath which still awakes a shame of sin and the gift of tears."

He enters into the dim aisles of a vast cathedral and listens to the magnificent music that the distant choir sings. The passage is a striking one:

"Durtal sat down again. The sweetness of his solitude was enhanced by the aromatic perfume of wax and the memories, now faint, of incense, but it was suddenly broken. As the first chords crashed on the organ Durtal recognized the *Dies Iræ*, that despairing hymn of the Middle Ages; instinctively he bowed his head and listened.

"This was no more, as in the *De Profundis*, a humble supplication, a suffering which believes it has been heard, and discerns a path of light to guide it in the darkness, no longer the prayer which has hope enough not to tremble; it was the cry of absolute desolation and terror. And, indeed, the wrath divine breathed tempestuously through these stanzas. They seemed addressed less to the God of Mercy, to the Son who listens to prayer, than to the inflexible Father, to Him whom the Old Testament shows us overcome with anger, scarcely appeased by the smoke of the pyres

10

and the inconceivable attractions of burnt-offerings. In this chant it asserted itself still more savagely, for it threatened to strike the waters, and break in pieces the mountains, and to rend asunder the depths of heaven by thunder-bolts. And the earth, alarmed, cried out in fear.

" A crystalline voice, a clear, child's voice, proclaimed in the nave the tidings of these cataclysms, and after this the choir chanted new strophes wherein the implacable judge came with shattering blare of trumpet to purify by fire the rottenness of the world.

" Then, in its turn, a bass, deep as a vault, as though issuing from the crypt, accentuated the horror of these prophecies, made these threats more overwhelming; and after a short strain by the choir, an alto repeated them in still more detail.   Then, as soon as the awful poem had exhausted the enumeration of chastisement and suffering, in shrill tones—the falsetto of a little boy—the name of Jesus went by, and a light broke in upon the thunder-cloud, the panting universe cried for pardon, recalling, by all the voices of the choir, the infinite mercies of the Saviour, and His pardon, pleading with Him for absolution, as formerly He had spared the penitent thief and the Magdalen. But in the same despairing and headstrong melody the tempest raged again, drowned with its waves the half-seen shores of heaven, and the solos continued, discouraged, interrupted by the recurrent weeping of the choir, giving, with the diversity of voices, a body to the special conditions of shame, the particular states of fear, the different ages of tears.

" At last, when, still mixed and blended, these voices

had borne away on the great waters of the organ all
the wreckage of human sorrows, all the buoys of prayers and tears, they fell exhausted, paralyzed by terror,
wailing and sighing like a child who hides its face,
stammering *Dona eis requiem*, they ended, worn out,
in an Amen so plaintive that it died away in a breath
above the sobbing of the organ.

"What man could have imagined such despair or
dreamed of such disasters?   And Durtal made answer
to himself, ' No man.' "

In fact, Durtal was brought back to religion
by his love for art ; and the sight of the count-
less worshippers who knelt day after day before the crucifix shook to the depths his tainted soul.   He believed, and his whole being
cried out for a refuge from his disgust with
life, his infinite weariness of self.   But as yet
he had faith alone.   He could not pray ; he
could not even master the temptations of the
flesh that kept assailing him with even greater strength than heretofore.   He sinned and
sinned again, even while his mind was full of
these new emotions.   But at this moment he
fell under the influence of a priest, a shrewd,
kindly man, of vast experience, cultivated, and
a keen judge of human nature.   Him Durtal
consults, not as a priest so much as a sympathetic friend ; and little by little he yields to
the kindly influence of the shrewd old Abbé.

With infinite tact and delicate finesse the
Abbé leads him on to take an interest in those
orders in the Church that are purely contem-
plative—especially the Trappist branch of the
Cistercians.   Little by little Durtal's imagination is fired by the thought of a life of such
pure devotion, until at last the Abbé Gévresin
suggests that he spend a short time as a " retreatant " in the Trappist monastery of Notre
Dame de l'Atre, shut out from the world, and
surrounded by the influence and example of
those monks who approach in their lives the
nearest to complete self-abnegation.   Durtal is
startled at the thought.   He asks questions as
to the restraints that are imposed upon a layman who enters even for a week a monastery
such as this.   His first objections are singular
in their modernness.   He is fond of cigarettes,
and cannot think of giving up tobacco.   He
hates oily cookery, and he cannot digest milk
in any form.   But the notion of becoming a
retreatant fascinates him.   He reflects and hesitates.   It occurs to him that he can perhaps
find some way of smoking cigarettes by stealth
in the woods about the monastery.   He thinks
that he can stand the cooking.   At last, after
days of internal conflict, he decides to go, and
makes a prayer—a most curious prayer :

" Take count of this, O Lord : I know by experience
that when I am ill-fed I have neuralgia. Humanly,
logically speaking, I am certain to be horribly ill at
Notre Dame de l'Atre ; nevertheless, if I can get about
at all, the day after to-morrow I will go all the same.
In default of love, this is the only proof I can give that
I desire Thee, that I truly hope and believe in Thee ;
but do Thou, O Lord, aid me."

The same odd mixture of modernity and
mediævalism is seen throughout. Durtal, with
his mind filled by thoughts of St. Magdalen of
Pazzi and Bonaventura and Dionysius the Are-
opagite, stuffs his valise with pink packages of
cigarettes, and Menier's sweet chocolate, and
antipyrine, and sets out for the monastery
from the Gare du Nord. It is impossible to
give here even the briefest recapitulation of his
experiences, which Huysmans tells with minute
detail and the most extraordinary frankness.
His life as a retreatant, his spiritual struggles,
his mental battles with unbelief, his victories
and his defeats, are vivid in their realism. One
feels that this is just what would be the experience of a modern, only half-weaned from a
loose and lawless life, suddenly plunged into
an atmosphere of the strictest mediævalism.
This life keeps recurring to the imagination of
Durtal. A certain Florence comes to his mind

with maddening persistency. He sees continually her sly face aping the modesty of a little
girl, her slim body, her strange tastes that lead
her to drink toilet-scents and to eat caviare
with dates. Once he believes that Satan himself enters the room and fills it with visions of
horror. Again, in the midst of prayer, he is
seized with a fearful longing to rise and yell
out blasphemies. He finally goes to confession,
and the scene is told with curious minuteness.
Then at last a great calm comes upon him.
The atmosphere of intense devotion, the sublime reality of the faith that inspires all about
him, their life devoted to the single end of
praise and worship and adoration, and the
benignant and sympathetic kindness of the
monks soothe and comfort and strengthen
him. Here are rest and hope and perfect
tranquillity; and the book ends with his regret-
ful return to Paris and the expression of his
longing for a life of religious contemplation.

" If they [his loose companions] knew how inferior
they are to the lowest of the lay brothers! If they
could imagine how the divine intoxication of a Trappist interests me more than all their conversations and
all their books! Ah, Lord, that I might live, live in
the shadow of the prayers of humble Brother Simeon!"

En Route is interesting in many ways. It is

unique among the other books of Huysmans
in style no less than in spirit. Here he has
wholly put aside the studied bareness and
hardness of expression that characterize his
earlier method, and the descriptive passages
glow with color and abound in strange felicities
of expression. His enthusiasm for the purely
mediæval fairly carries him away, and I think
has led him into indefensible extremes. Did
space permit we should like to say something
of his evident devotion to plain song as against
the harmonized Gregorian chant of Palestrina,
for I think that the greatest masters of church
music would decline to follow him in his lack
of discrimination between the plain song in the
Prefaces to the Mass and in the other portions
of the service where more than a single voice
is necessary for the full effect. His enthusiasm
leads him also into long and rather tedious
digressions upon the history of the mediæval
saints, whose lives he insists upon detailing
with remorseless elaboration, so that the effect
produced is thoroughly inartistic from a literary point of view, and gives the impression of
one who has crammed up a subject and is un-
willing to lose any portion of his material.

Interesting also is the psychological side of
the book, with its implied thesis that faith, like

all other emotions, is contagious; and with its
illustration of the thought with which I com-
menced this paper, that the sensual nature
under certain influences can become the most
profoundly spiritual and religious.   M. Huysmans is usually classified as one of the disciples
of Émile Zola; but Zola could never have
written a book like this, for, in spite of the
contrary opinion that prevails, Zola is no sensualist, in the fullest meaning of the word.
He is only an intense materialist, and he lacks
a sympathetic insight into phenomena that
are purely spiritual.   He is like the photogra-
pher who, with equal unconcern and as a matter of mere business, will in the same hour turn
his camera upon the dead child in its coffin
filled with flowers, or upon the leering dancer
in her spangled tights.

To those of us who are Protestants the book
is full of deep instruction in revealing with
startling force the secret of the power of that
wonderful religious organization which has
made provision for the needs of every human
soul, whether it requires for its comfort active
service or the mystical life of contemplation.
We see how every want is understood and how
for every spiritual problem an answer is provided; how the experience of twenty centuries

has been stored up and recorded, and how all that man has ever known is known to those who guide and perpetuate this mighty system. And in these days when Doctors of Divinity devote their energies to nibbling away the foundations of historic faith, and when the sharpest weapons of agnosticism are forged on theological anvils, there is something reassuring in the contemplation of the one great Church that does not change from age to age, that stands unshaken on the rock of its convictions, and that speaks to the wavering and troubled soul in the serene and lofty accents of divine authority.

THE PASSING OF NORDAU

THE PASSING OF NORDAU

IT must seem a little curious to many readers of current literature that Max Nordau's ponderous indictment of modern civilization has so soon and so completely passed into the limbo of half-forgotten things. There was a moment when it appeared as though a great light had flashed upon the dark corners of society, displaying abysmal depths of foulness and corruption lying all about us; as though for an instant there had been revealed a ghastly spectre hovering over the modern world and, like the Erl-King of German legend, reaching out a hideous paw to destroy all that is dearest and holiest in the lives of mortal men. To-day, while in the remoter parts of the country *Degeneration* has probably its share of startled readers, the world at large has ceased to think of it; and its portentous pages have left no mark behind them save the addition of a few phrases to the literary slang of the time, and perhaps a deeper taint upon the morbid imagination of a few disordered minds. What appeared for the moment to be the voice of one crying in the wilderness to prepare the social cosmos for the damnation that was sure to come, is now very clearly seen to have been merely a well-timed though unwholesome and spasmodic literary sensation.

It is the strange rapidity and completeness of this decline of interest in Nordau's fulminations that make the various volumes written to refute his arguments appear almost as antiquated as an attack on Fourierism or as a serious polemic against the Millerite delusion. Thinking men have taken Nordau's measure. They have analyzed his utterances, and examined his facts, and tested the logic of his deductions; and as a result of their examination they have laid his book aside and turned to other and more profitable themes.

It is, of course, from one point of view, unfair to drag into a discussion the personality of a writer in estimating the value of his theses, for this sort of thing is bound to smack of the argument *ad hominem;* yet in the case of Herr Nordau it is impossible not to reflect upon his character and temperament as revealed in all his published work; for a knowledge of these things has undoubtedly contributed to minimize the influence of his book. Moreover, one need feel no great compunction in speaking of him very frankly, for in *Degeneration* he has erected a whole mountain of theory upon his own estimate of living men, and has taken it upon himself in the most offhand fashion to define their motives and to question their sincerity. And when his book was flung before the eyes of the Anglo-Saxon world, the first question asked on every hand was, "Who is Nordau?"

A quick-witted Jew, imbued, like many of his race to-day, with an impenetrable materialism, a sceptic and yet a doctrinaire, Nordau is less an individual than a type, and a type raised to the *n*th. For him the world of spirit has absolutely no existence, the altruistic motive no force, ideal beauty no reality. Trained to study the perversities of the phenomena that are revealed to the alienist, tracing everything to a physical source, and accepting to the full the theories of his master, Lombroso, he is an ideal illustration of the credulity of science. He cannot believe in imagination save as a symptom of irrationality ; he cannot recognize any love of beauty save as a manifestation of erotomania. Yet he can worship physiology as a clue to all the mysteries of

life, and think himself able to sound the very
depths of the human soul by measuring men's
ears and noting down the conformation of
their frontal bones.   From the earliest days
of his student life he seems to have had a
strangely morbid curiosity as to the abnormal.
He pried into all the dark corners of diseased
mentality; he collected all the prurient details
of the psychiatrist's practice; and with an avid
delight he gleaned in the remotest fields of
sexual psychopathy.   The few unhappy creatures who in another age would have raved behind the bars of a mad-house, but whom the
printing-press has given to-day a speaking-tube
to reach the public ear, Nordau watches with
the joy of a connoisseur, jotting down in a
note-book every fearful phrase, and garnering
up every perverse, disjointed thought.   He
wades through whole libraries, to wrench from
its context any bit of reprehensible description and add it to his collection.   Presently
he has volumes upon volumes of this sort of
stuff; he has haunted the hospitals and asy-
lums, and made for himself a little world of
his own, peopled by the ghastly figures of the
diseased, the dying, and the degenerate; and
then at last he comes out into the greater
world—the world of sunlight and sanity—with

a mind that has itself become perverted, a
mind that has lost its sense of proportion, and
has grown intellectually color-blind. He has
so accustomed himself to watching for telltale
symptoms that he sees them on every side,
even in the healthiest mind and the soundest
body. The slightest coincidences are to him
conclusive evidence of identity; and he puts his
own hideous interpretation upon everything
that meets his view, until, as has been very
truly said, he is himself an abnormality and a
pathological type. Every large hospital for
the insane knows his representative—the one
sane man in a world of lunatics. Yet there is
a very apparent method in his madness. He
has a canny, commercial side to him that is extremely characteristic of his race; and seeing
that certain topics are attracting some attention, and that the world is ready for a new
sensation, he infers that the psychological
moment has arrived; and at once, gathering up
his ponderous note-books, he compacts them
into a bulky volume, garnishes them with a
pseudo-scientific sauce, cooks up a theory to
justify his exposure, and launches the delect-
able combination upon an appreciative market.

Probably the strongest proof of the falsity

11

of Nordau's view of society is to be found
in the sensation which his book created; for
this sensation was not that which springs from
startled conviction and guilty recognition, but
from sheer astonishment and incredulity.   It
was the shock which might be felt by a traveller who, walking quietly along a pleasant
road, should find his way blocked by a mighty
avalanche of muck.   At first he might believe
that here was some great cataclysm, some wonderful phenomenon of nature; but a moment's
inspection would speedily convince him that,
after all, it was muck, and nothing more.   And
so with Nordau's book.   The world wondered
for a moment, because the world at large had
never even dreamed that such things as Nordau
wrote of were in existence.   Thousands of intelligent men and women had never so much
as heard the names of Huysmans and Nietz-
sche and Paul Verlaine.   The subtleties of the
Symbolists were unknown to them.   They had
innocently looked upon Wagner as a great
master of dramatic music, upon Ruskin as a
refined and stimulating critic, upon Tolstoi as
a powerful novelist and a sincere if impractica-
ble humanitarian.   And as to the darker and
more repellent facts set forth by Nordau from
the treatises of Krafft-Ebing and other special-

ists in neuropathy, of these things they had never even had an inkling. Therefore, just as the traveller described above, after looking for a moment at the muck-heap, would simply hold his nose and pass around it, so Nordau's readers, after a very short consideration of his pages, metaphorically held their noses and turned away from the further contemplation of his pornographic pile.

Some few, however, interested in the abnormality of the whole thing, lingered for a while to investigate it in a scientific spirit; and these speedily found good reasons for the contempt which was with the world at large a matter of unerring instinct and intuition. They at once detected the unreality and fundamental unimportance of it all. They noted the singular perversity that deduced from every intellectual product of the age one and the same conclusion; that called one man a maniac because he wrote so much, and another man a maniac because he wrote so little; that set down still another as an incipient criminal because his ears were said to be pointed at the ends, and a fourth as subject to "echolalia" because his verse abounds in cadenced repetitions; that in one place declared human beings too good and noble to need the fear of hell,

and in another place described them as too vile
to dispense with the fear of the gallows and
the hangman.

They noted him saying that material success
in life is a test of sound-mindedness, and yet
considering just how far the same success is
evidence of degeneracy. They saw him also,
with a subtlety of erotic suggestion, detecting
sexuality in what all men before him had seen
nothing but the beauty and the joy of art, and
infusing a lingering taint into some of the
noblest creations of the human imagination.
Finally, they turned to what Nordau had himself produced in the sphere of fiction, and there
finding writ large the sordid sensuality which
he had wantonly ascribed to the masters of
modern literature, they at once convicted him
beyond the possibility of defence of all that he
had claimed to see in others. It needed only
a clear appreciation of these things to discredit
and refute the whole elaborate attack that he
had made upon the age ; and when it was quite
plainly understood that the author of *Degeneration* was himself simply a stray degenerate,
raving with foul words at his environment, all
interest in him, save as in an abnormal type,
at once declined.

To my mind the most forceful and truly il-

luminative comment on his book is that in
which the anonymous author of a recent volume called *Regeneration* traces in Nordau's work
and in his mental attitude the influence of a
powerful German bias, and which sets forth in
very vigorous and convincing language the essential traits of the typical German. A single
sentence will suffice to give the reader a clue
to his argument :

> "German education and German surroundings tend
> to foster in the human mind veneration for authority,
> contempt for the plebeian, distrust of liberty, a firm
> belief in the unquenchable power of man's lowest in-
> stincts, a nervous demand for authoritative repression
> of human passions, and contentment with prosaic ex-
> istence, small resources, and poor prospects."

How true this is and how far-reaching is the
truth in its practical manifestations, every one
who has lived in Germany, or who has studied
German character as mirrored in German history and in the social characteristics of the
German people, must be profoundly conscious.
The typical German is a being who, if he gives
play to the higher and more creative impulses
at all, does so only in the sphere of imagination, while his actual life is dominated by the
most intense materialism. A pure sentimen-

talist, his thought and his action have apparently no relation whatever to each other.   He con-
templates with intellectual enthusiasm the ideal
beauty, and he lives contented with the most
squalid environment. He worships ideal purity,
and he indulges himself in methodical sensuality.   He writes lachrymose verse imbued with
chivalrous sentiment for woman, and then he
yokes his wife with a dog or an ass and sets
her ploughing in his potato-fields.   He can describe on paper an elaborate Utopia of justice
and political perfection, and he is governed by
one of the rankest and most brutal despotisms
that ever smothered human freedom under the
bonds of a military bureaucracy.   Hence it is
that the Germans, with all their training and
all their many admirable traits, are lacking in
constructiveness, in spontaneity, in creative
boldness.   When things go wrong, and when
an American or an Englishman would take his
coat off and set them right by the vigor and
originality of his native energy, a German
rolls up his eyes helplessly and begins to whim-
per for some higher power to tell him what
to do.   A curious indication of this national
proneness to despair is seen in the fact that of
all the suicides recorded in our daily press by
far the greater number is that of men and

women with German names. And this is why
the history of Germany is what it is—a history
of divided and discordant principalities, of a
people submitting to the rule of a hundred
petty despots, unable to do more than maunder
over the liberty that none of them would
strike a blow to win ; of a people who forgot at
Napoleon's bidding their national self-respect,
and fought his battles for him against their
own kindred and natural allies.   In 1848 they
had a chance to show what they could do at
constructing a parliamentary government, and
they produced nothing but a windy debating
society of visionary doctrinaires, to be soon
dismissed contemptuously by a military prince.
When some strong, masterful spirit arises
among them—a man like Frederick the Great
or Bismarck—they do not use him as a national instrument, but he sets his foot on all their
necks and forces them to do his bidding.
Hence it is that Germany presents to-day the
astounding spectacle of a nation, the most
highly educated in the world, governed by
drill-sergeants and sub-lieutenants, accepting a
régime that makes it a penal offence to speak
disrespectfully of an artillery - mule, and in
which the best born, the most eminent, and
the most highly trained all flock with enthusias-

tic self-abasement to lick the jack-boots of a
pinchbeck Cæsar.

It is quite reasonable, therefore, to recognize
in Nordau's book a true reflection of the German temperament. The pedantic marshalling
of documentary evidence to convict whole
nations, the intellectual near-sightedness that
sees no further than the hospital and the dis-
secting-room and that knows nothing of the
play of forces in the greater world beyond,
the moral cowardice, the negation of hope, the
grossness of the materialism, the suspicious
distrust, the attempt to reduce the things of
the spirit to an unvarying formula—surely
these are not the traits of the broad-minded,
far-seeing, and sane philosopher. They suggest rather the Herr Professor in his stuffy
study, evolving from his books and from his
inner consciousness a theory for interminable
exploitation in the lecture - room. Nordau's
whole work, in fact, came bearing the ear-marks
of a nation that regards an intelligent machine
as the perfection of human progress, that finds
in every vista an *impasse*, and that sees in every
paltry mole-hill the menace of a mighty mountain.

But what is one to say of Nordau's main
contention that our age is marked with the

stigmata of degeneracy? Is the world really
growing better or is it growing worse? Probably the serious student of social phenomena
would say that in reality there is little actual
gain from one generation to another, but that
in all ages and among all civilized peoples the
sum total of essential morality remains unchanged. At one period some particular vice
or some particular virtue will be in the ascendant, and at another period another. In early
Rome, for instance, chastity and personal honesty were the rule, yet they were accompanied
by an utter lack of humanity and of the softer
virtues. A wife could be beaten to death for
drinking wine ; Cato could order an innocent
slave to be slain merely to impress the other
serfs with their master's power. Under the
Empire such cruelty became impossible, yet
the growth of the sentiment of mercy was coincident with a decline of integrity and of
sexual morality. And so, too, in the case of
contemporaneous peoples, neither the especial
vice nor the especial virtue of the one is necessarily that of the other. There is no doubt,
for instance, that the standard of commercial
morality is appreciably higher in England than
in the United States, and that the laws of
property are held to be more sacred there than

here ; but, on the other hand, the brute who
in England kicks his wife with heavy clogs
gets off with a small fine, while to all men is
permitted a degree of license in the sphere
of personal morality which if practised here
would insure an instant ostracism.

And so the balance is apparently kept even.
Yet, after all, the impartial student of manners,
who looks back over the pages of history and
the record of men's lives, can scarcely fail to
perceive with every cycle a certain steady progress that is not merely onward, but upward too.
The dark side of the picture is not quite so
dark as it was once, and the bright side is far
brighter.   The standards of virtue are, at any
rate, accepted now by all men, and acceptance
must ultimately mean observance also.   Humanity moves onward with a stumbling step
and many a halt, yet it does advance, and with
every century its gaze is fixed with an increas-
ing steadiness upon the lofty and immutable
ideals of justice and mercy and purity and
truth.

THE MIGRATION OF POPULAR SONGS

THE MIGRATION OF POPULAR SONGS

LEST the reader should find, as he easily might, some ambiguity in the title of this short paper, it may be well to explain, by way of premise, that popular songs are here taken to mean only the songs of the day, ephemeral, trivial, and of little or no musical value — the songs that spring up, as it were, in a night, that are sung and whistled and played for a few weeks or months, and are then forgotten. The songs that endure for generations, though often of no greater intrinsic merit, are more truly described as national songs; for the national song is by no means necessarily one whose words and music, or even the circumstances of whose composition, are associated with an historical or patriotic event. The *Ranz des Vaches*, for instance, is most truly the national air of Switzerland, though it is only a herdsman's strain; and Bayard Taylor's poem keeps alive the fact that on the eve of the bloodiest battle of the Crimean War the Scotch regiments fed their martial spirit by singing, not the stirring music of their grandest battle-hymn, *Scots wha hae*, but the simple strains of *Annie Laurie*. Just what gives vitality to some of these songs it is hard to say ; but the fact is plain enough that while most of them pass out of memory within a year, a few express in some subtle way the deeper feelings of a nation and live throughout the rest of its history.   Thus *Partant pour la Syrie*, and *Ça Ira*, and the *Carmagnole*, and *Yankee Doodle*, and *Marching Through Georgia* will outlive the French and American republics, while *En R'v'nant de la Revue*, and *Père la Victoire*, and *Just Before the Battle*, and *We Don't Want to Fight* are forgotten in a single generation.   And the reason for the immortality of the one set and for the oblivion of the other is about equally mysterious.

The popular song, however, in the restricted sense of the word — the song of the whistling boy and the street-piano — is at present often able to secure a brief respite from immediate forgetfulness, to cheat oblivion, and secure a second lease of life by a species of migration.

In these days, when travel is cheap and when each nation, being more or less informed about

its neighbor's doings, finds it an amusing thing
to be imitative and cosmopolitan, the popular
song is one of the objects that, like food, fashions, and literature, are amiably borrowed.
Thus it happens that when some ditty has
become such a nuisance in the land of its
birth as to make its public rendition more or
less unsafe, it suddenly disappears, and almost
immediately reappears in some other country,
where it is treated as an attractive novelty.
When it springs up again in this way among
a people whose language is not that of its
author, it often suffers a sea-change; but the
music is usually unaltered, while the transformation of its words is often very characteristic
and amusing.

One would say *a priori* that England and
America would be the greatest borrowers of
the *chansonette*. As Germany is the most
musical land in the world, and as France is
the home of the *café chantant*, it might be
supposed that the English "music-hall" and
the American "variety show" would find the
French and German airs an inexhaustible store
to borrow from. But the truth of the matter
is quite the reverse, and for two very different
reasons. As regards Germany, it is precisely
because the Germans are so musical that the

foreign conveyer of popular songs finds so
little to appropriate. The German's taste in
music is so educated and he takes his music
so seriously, as to make nonsense-songs, such
as those of our country and of England, appear to him neither amusing nor agreeable.
They are simply monstrosities, fit only for eccentric and Philistine nations, such as he sup-
poses us to be. The Tingeltangel plays no
such important part in the economy of his
amusements as does the *café chantant* in the
diversions of the French. When he listens to
music, it must be good in itself. The difference is well seen in such an establishment as
Kroll's Garten, in Berlin—a place in many respects akin to the Folies Bergère, of Paris. It
is an immense beer-garden; yet its open-air
music is rendered by a really fine orchestra,
supplemented occasionally by some of the
military bands of the garrison; while in the
adjacent theatre appear singers of international celebrity, who interpret the *rôles* of the
lighter of the grand operas, such as the *Meis-
tersinger*, the *Trompeter von Säkingen*, and *The
Flying Dutchman*. In fact, the German seldom descends to any lower depth, musically,
than the comic opera; and when an American,
an Englishman, or a Frenchman would be hum-

ming *The Band Played On* or *Gigolette*, a German contents himself with a bit of Millöcker or Suppé—something far from classical, if you will, but by no means cheap and vulgar. And as he does not himself produce our sort of popular song, still less does he import those which we have made. Some of Gilbert and Sullivan's comic operas he will tolerate (the airs from the *Mikado* were rather popular in Germany at one time), and Mr. Reginald De Koven is not unknown ; but that is the limit of his toleration. It is true that in the numerous Tingeltangels our comic songs are often heard, but they are sung in their original form by foreign singers, English and American, and are listened to by the Germans in the same spirit in which a visitor to Chinatown enjoys the performance of a Mongolian orchestra. Hence our purveyors of popular music find nothing of the kind in Germany to appropriate ; but with true American audacity they have gone straight to the classical music, and from it have filched innumerable themes. It may not be generally known, for instance, that the chorus of *Oh, How I Love My Ada* is taken bodily from the overture to *Zanetta*, that the chorus of *Paradise Alley* is an echo of the drinking-song in *Cavalleria Rusticana*, that

12

Annie Rooney is taken directly, with a mere change of *tempo*, from a chorale of Bach ; and that *Down went McGinty* is stolen from another. It is an amusing fact that Wagner derived the so-called bell-motif in *Parsifal* from the last-named source ; so that we have the great master of modern music drinking from the same fountain of inspiration as the author of *Down went McGinty!*

Again, not very much is borrowed from the French. The reason for this is to be found, I think, in the musical characteristics of the French *chansonettes*. The French popular music is eminently vivacious ; it has a sort of sparkle that is distinctly Gallic ; but there is something about it that makes it rather unattractive to an English ear. It is too jerky ; it lacks rhythm and melody ; and it does not easily fix itself in the memory. It is, in fact, rather thin, and irresistibly suggests the nasal tones and cracked pianos of the *gargotes* through which it finally passes into oblivion. Hence it is not often borrowed, the exceptions being found principally in semimilitary songs. These are occasionally transplanted to England and America, though they are there not sung, but arranged for military bands and for orchestras. An instance of this

is the Boulangist chant, *En R'v'nant de la Revue*, first sung by Paulus at the Alcazar d'Été,
and speedily taken up all over France by the
partisans of the *brav' Général*. It was at
once *cabled* to this country (a journalistic
feat achieved by the New York *Herald*), and
was heard everywhere, but only as an air, no
words ever having been written for it in English, so far as I know. A later French success,
Père la Victoire, likewise "created" by Paulus
at the Eldorado, was at one time a good deal
played by military bands in England, where it
was also set to new words; but as a song it had
no success. Therefore, the fact remains that
while we borrow French fashions, French
cookery, French plays, and French novels,
the Anglo-Saxon world cares very little for
French popular songs.

Equally unsuccessful has proved the attempt
to adapt for English and American use any of
the numerous *canzonette* of Italy, and for the
same reasons. Perhaps the last attempt to
make a hit in this way was that of Miss Lot-
tie Collins, who, after the song which is especially associated with her name had been
worn threadbare, announced with a good deal
of journalistic trumpeting a new one entitled
Marguerite of Monte Carlo. This was in real-

ity an English adaptation of a Neapolitan *canzone* by the popular song-writer Piedigrotta, first sung at the Salone Margherita in Naples in 1892, when it caught the fancy of the populace immensely, and was soon sung, whistled, and played all over Italy.   The original was called *Margarita de Parete*, and was written in dialect.   It has a good deal of swing to it, but in spite of Miss Collins's own popularity, and her persistent efforts to make it a success, it fell rather flat, and never reached the street-piano.

Not many of our popular airs, then, are foreign ; but a very great many of ours are caught up by the French, especially those songs whose English words have a jingle that tickles the Gallic ear with a suggestion of eccentricity. Such, for example, is an absurd but rather tuneful ditty, once much in vogue in England, though never very well known in this country, and entitled *Linger Longer, Loo*. The original is by Messrs. Young and Sidney Jones, and it so amused the first Frenchman who heard it that it was almost immediately carried to Paris.   French words were written by M. Henri Dreyfus, the English chorus being retained, and it was sung by no less a personage than the famous Yvette Guilbert, and later by Mlle. Duclerc at the Folies Bergère.   The first

verse of the French rendering will give a good
idea of *le genre Anglaisiste*, so called :

> Ça n'vous amuse pas c'que j' dis là
> Moi non plus je l'atteste,
> Mais il faut bien par ci par là,
> Chanter de tout et l'reste.
> Mon répertoire est folichon
> A c'que dis'nt les familles
> Aussi ma p'tite *English* chanson
> Est fait' pour les jeunes filles.
> Leurs papas diront c'est plus beau
> Bien qu' vous n' compreniez pas un mot,
> Ell's pens'ront, sûr, y'a pas d'plaisir
> Du moment qu'on n' peut pas rougir !

> "*Linger longer, Lucy, linger longer, Loo,*
> *How I love to linger, Lucy, linger long o' you ;*
> *Listen while I sing, ah, tell me you'll be true,*
> *Linger longer, longer linger, linger longer, Loo !*"

The Man that Broke the Bank at Monte Carlo
was a great favorite with the French, and their
version of it was a close paraphrase of the English, though it very characteristically represented the breaker of the bank as a woman,
and not a man. The title of it was *J'ai fait
sauter la banque à Monte Carlo*. As a rule, the
music alone is taken, the French words having
no reference to the original ones. Thus, *Daisy
Bell*, or, as the French usually wrote it. *Daysey*

Bell, furnished the music for a rather amusing set of verses by M. Dreyfus, who is an Anglophobe, in which *les Anglaises pour rire* are vigorously mocked—their diet of *bifteck*, *rumsteck*, and other *viandes saignantes*, their prudery, and their dress. A verse may serve to amuse the reader.

A Paris va des Anglaises
    L'air sec, avec
Des appas comm' des punaises
Des dents longu's et jaun's dans l'bec.
Sur l' boul'vard chacun' circule
Vêtu' comm' d'un foureau
D'un *macfarlan'* ridicule
Coiffé' d'un tout p'tit chapeau !

All right! All right!
Rien ne les emotionne ;
All right! All right!
Rien ne les passionne ;
Ell's ont la sech'ress' d'un' planche,
Ell's ont aussi sa raideur,
Que c'soit la s'maine ou l'dimanche
Un rien offense leur pioudeur !

The chorus of this had almost as much success in France as the original enjoyed in England and the United States; and up to the present time, when a *gamin* wishes to jeer at a stray Englishman, he greets him with the

" All right !" which, together with " Aôh yes !"
is regarded in France as the shibboleth of the
Anglo-Saxon race.

As might be expected, *Tarara-boom-de-ay* exactly suited the *Anglaisistes*. It had scarcely
appeared in England and America before a
French rendering was rushed into print, in fact
so rapidly that the author of it, M. Fabrice
Lémon, failed to notice the exact title of the
original and altered a syllable, his version bearing the name *Tha-mara-boum-di-hé ;* but it was
a great success, being sung at one and the
same time at four of the principal *cafés con-
certs*—the Alcazar, the Horloge, the Ambas-
sadeurs, and the Folies Bergère.   Before, however, any French version at all had been made,
the present writer, being in a provincial town
in Normandy, read one day an announcement
of the local theatre to the effect that on the
following evening a new one-act play would be
presented, with the remarkable title *Miss Kiss-
my*, in which the forward manners of the typical *mees Anglaise* would be held up to the rep-
robation of a virtuous French audience.   It
was also announced as a special attraction that
a certain Mlle. Dufort would, in the course of
the play, sing the *célèbre chanson Anglaise,
Tha-ra-ra-boum-der-é*.   When the time came

and Mlle. Dufort appeared she had an immense
audience.   The first few lines made it evident
(not to the audience, however) that this ingenious young woman had shrunk from the task
of "getting up" the lines of the genuine version, but had instead constructed a set of
verses of her own by piecing together all the
English words she had ever heard.   The first
verse, then, ran something like this :

> Ticket tramway clergyman
> Bifteck rumsteck rosbif van,
> Sandwich whitebaits lady lunch
> Chéri-gobler, wiskey-ponche ;
> Aôh-yes all right shocking stop
> Pêl-êl why-not moton-chop,
> Plum-kêk miousic steamer boxe,
> Boule-dogue high-life five-o'clocks.
>   Tha-ra-ra-boum-der-é, etc.

It was an immense success.   The audience
rose at her.   They knew that the English was
all right, because they themselves recognized
a good many of the words.   She had an ova-
tion and nine encores; and this was probably
the first rendition of the *célèbre chanson* on
French soil.

It has already been noted that the French,
in taking over the English popular songs, seldom or never translate the words literally.

The reason of this is very characteristic.   In
the first place, the French mind is too logically
reasonable to relish mere nonsense such as delights with a childish joy a typical Anglo-Saxon
audience.   Possibly the Gallic lack of humor
also stands in the way of an appreciation of
pure absurdity.   In the second place, the French
have an innate literary instinct that demands
precision, neatness of phrasing, and point, in
even the lightest verses to which they are asked
to listen ; and the commonplaces of our sentimental ballads are to them indescribably inane.
Hence in the lines that they write for our popular music there are to be found almost always
a wit and a meaning to which the English
words have no claim.   Yet in another way
the balance is in our favor ; for an unpleasant
French trait almost always mars their verses—
the fondness for striking the note of the un-
cleanly suggestive.   Our English words may
be utterly nonsensical, their sentiment may be
commonplace and its expression mawkish, yet
both words and sentiment are clean and wholesome ; the nonsense is good, honest nonsense,
and one never carries away, after listening to
it, an unpleasant taste ; and this quality in our
popular songs and popular singers is far better
than all the tainted wit of a Dreyfus and a

Baneux, and the inspired *diablerie* of Yvette
Guilbert and Duhamel. A good instance of
how the French bedevil an innocent piece of
fun can be seen by comparing the English
popular song *Ting-a-ling* with the French version called *Ling-a-ling*, first sung by Edmée
Lescot at the Casino de Paris. The English
is a rollicking bit of harmless nonsense; but
of the French version there is not a single
stanza that I should venture to reprint.

There is one thing which seems quite remarkable in the popular songs of the French to-day,
and which has a deep significance of its own.
When we reflect upon the fact that France is
now in reality a great armed camp, that its
people are waiting with a feverish anxiety—
an intense feeling of hope and fear—for the
inevitable hour when they shall strike the great
blow to avenge the humiliation of 1870; when
one remembers how intensely martial is the
spirit of the whole nation, how it is yearning
for its old supremacy and for the glory that
was dimmed at Gravelotte and Sedan, and at
the same time recalls how effusive the French
temperament is, it is simply marvellous to find
the singers of the people's songs so silent on
the one theme that lies closest to every patriotic Frenchman's heart. No ballads revile the

hated Prussian; no martial songs call for the
hastening of the day of reckoning; no new
Béranger puts into the lyrics of the street the
fierce longing that throbs in the pulses of so
many millions. This very silence, ominous,
universal, is the most profoundly impressive
evidence of the intensity of the flame that
needs no outward fanning to keep it in a glow.
"The shallows murmur, but the deeps are
dumb"; and the underlying thought seems
to be this: that to recall the horrors of 1870
would be humiliating, unbearable; while to
sing of what all hope for in the future would
be only to play the braggart's part in the face
of possibilities that make the lightest spirit
shrink back with awe from their contemplation.

I have said that there is scarcely a trace in
any popular song of the spirit of *revanche;* yet
here and there a word, a phrase, or a turn of
expression reveals it as by a flash. One of the
most striking illustrations of this, and perhaps
the boldest, is found in the *Marche des Treize
Jours*, a song that was sung all over France
not very long ago. It is professedly only a
comic song, narrating the amusing experiences
of a *réserviste* who goes into camp to perform
his thirteen days of required military service;
but the last verse strikes a different note:

Quand les treiz' jours sont terminés
L'général nous dit : " J' vous r'mercie,
Vous êtes dign's de vos aînés !
A l'appel sacré de la Patrie
        Tous vous viendrez
        Et me direz :

" ' Les Treize Jours ne tremblent pas !
    Pour repousser les hordes étrangères
    Nous saurons tous dans les combats
    Nous battr' comm' de vieux militaires ! ' "
    Puis nous montrant notre drapeau,
  " Sachez mourir," dit-il, " pour sa défense !"
    Et l'général élevant son chapeau,
    Nous dit " À bientôt ! Vive la France !"

There is a world of meaning to every French-man in that *à bientôt !*

Another of the recent popular songs in France is also very significant—this one not for its words, but for its music. It is a song that I have already mentioned—*Père la Victoire*—first sung by Paulus at the Eldorado in the winter of 1891-92. The words are noth-ing — the revery of an old soldier — but the music, arranged by Louis Ganne for military bands, is in its way a wonderfully effective thing—a sort of cantata, whose meaning all France interpreted at once. It opens with a roll of drums and a trumpet-call, as heralding

the military character of its *motif*. Then comes
a long strain of melancholy music, sombre, pathetic, rising almost into a wail, though still
marked by the military accent. To the listener
it depicts France in her humiliation, beaten to
her knees by the merciless invader, betrayed,
despairing. Then, as the music almost dies
away, the muffled drums roll steadily, and a
firmer note is struck. France lives! The years
of patience, of sacrifice, of preparation have
come. Stronger and clearer the music swells
again into a noble march, majestic, confident,
courageous. Clearer and bolder ring out the
notes, faster and faster and richer and grander
are the harmonies. France is once more herself, puissant, girt for battle, invincible. The
hour has struck, and a storm of drums over-
whelms the ear in a great crash of martial
melody, with the trumpets once more ringing
out, this time exultant in the fierce joy of victory! It is the musical apotheosis of *la revanche*. Professional musicians may call it a
poor thing; but when rendered by a fine military band, as I have often heard it, it has always seemed to me inexpressibly thrilling; and
with its hidden meanings it must quicken the
pulse and stir the blood of every one who loves
France and her chivalrous people.

THE NEW CHILD AND ITS PICTURE-
BOOKS

THE NEW CHILD AND ITS PICTURE-BOOKS

AN ingenious person of great eminence in educational theory, but one whose patience is evidently more highly developed than his sense of humor, has been making some experiments that are supposed to be very important to scientific teachers. He has found that it takes a young child $\frac{364}{1000}$ of a second to recognize the letter c, $\frac{358}{1000}$ of a second to recognize the letter a, and $\frac{382}{1000}$ of a second to recognize the letter t; while the word c-a-t as a whole is recognized in $\frac{339}{1000}$ of a second. Therefore, he says, all primary teaching should be done by words and not by letters, and the words should be $\frac{1}{12}$ of an inch high and printed in a line not more than four inches long. One doesn't see exactly how he has discovered all these things, but that does not matter; for he is evidently a very profound person. I have done some figuring myself on the basis of his researches, and I find that, following out his

13

method and adopting his kind of reading-book, a child of five years, in an average daily lesson, would each day save $\frac{9789}{10000}$ of a minute out of its valuable time. Think of that!

This investigation is beautifully illustrative of what is going on to-day in the sphere of education. We are living in an age in which the Educator has been gradually supplanted by the Educationist. The Educator was a person who felt that every child has its own individual temperament and mental idiosyncrasies which differentiate it to some extent from every other child, so that the method of presenting a subject should be largely influenced by the teacher's knowledge of the individual to be taught. He felt that a good teacher should be quick to note the effects upon each child's mind of a particular manner of presentation, and that the practical results obtained should be the final test of every method, inasmuch as the education of the child and not the exaltation of the teacher was the end to be secured. Hence quick sympathy, keen perception, ready adaptability, and ingenuity in fixing the attention and interesting the thought of the child were regarded as the prime qualifications of a successful Educator.

The Educationist has changed all that. So far as my own limited intelligence has been able to grasp the subtle distinction of modern pædagogic doctrine, an Educationist is an individual who is not himself much of a hand at teaching, but who is able to tell all other persons how they ought to teach. He is great on method, and observes blandly, when questioned, that it doesn't matter in the least whether the actual results amount to much so long as the correct pædagogic method has been employed. He abounds in statistics, and these statistics are usually in fractions. He perhaps could not himself succeed in teaching a young child to read, but, like the *c-a-t* investigator, he can tell you just how many thousandths of a second it ought to take for some one else to make a letter perceptible to the child's intelligence. He has read several text-books on Psychology, and when he talks, he has a good deal to say about "concepts" and "apperception," and once in five minutes he will airily allude to the Laws of the Association of Ideas. He has, in fact, established a set of infallible formulas that never hang fire, and that render the education of children as simple a matter as rolling off a log. The exactness of these formulas is, indeed, a little startling to an ordinary mind. Thus, if the Educationist tells you that a child of twelve years and six months who is studying Latin must have exactly thirty-five minutes of recitation each day (preferably between nine and eleven o'clock), and you say doubtfully that you have been giving thirty minutes to this work between eleven and twelve o'clock, the Educationist will look at you with a pained surprise and tell you that you are evidently quite old fashioned. Then it would be wise to keep quiet unless you want to get into trouble ; for if you go on to say that your arrangement has worked very well, he will at once remark that you evidently know nothing of the Psychological Basis of Education ; and if you still persist, he will talk to you about Sturm, and Herbart, and maybe even Fræbel ; and if he once pulls Fræbel on you, you are gone. It is quite unsafe, too, for you to comfort yourself with the thought that perhaps he doesn't know what he is talking about. You may think that he is by no means brilliant in his ordinary conversation, that he seems, in fact, in other matters to be rather dull ; and if you are exceptionally uninstructed and indiscreet, you may even go so far as to remark that he is evidently a good deal of an ass.

But just wait, and Nemesis will at last get after you. Some day or other you will see the Educationist reading a paper at a Teachers' Conference, and then you will know that he is really Great.

Now, so far as we are personally concerned, we don't care how much he goes raiding around in the field of education, and we shouldn't say a word about him if he stopped right there. Children will tumble up somehow or other even under the rule of an Educationist ; and after all, the real training of every human being comes largely from experience and from contact with his kind. Moreover, there is something to be said in behalf of the psychological racket. In these days of overcrowded professions there are hundreds of shallow young men and rattle-pated young women who would have to carry a hod or go and get married if a wise dispensation of Providence had not specially opened up to them this new and fruitful field, wherein they can earn comfortable salaries and much κῦδος without needing to possess anything more in the way of equipment than a few catchwords and the ability to keep a straight face when they hear each other talk.

Unfortunately, however, these people have

not remained contented with their original sphere of influence. Perhaps they are getting to be so numerous that they have begun to tread upon each other's heels. At any rate, they are now slopping over into another field, in which they are doing and will continue to do an infinite deal of harm. After grabbing the schools and coercing the teachers, they are now reaching out into the nursery and into the playground, and are seeking to upset all the good old traditions of child-life that have come down from the time when the Aryan children romped around on the borders of Volhynia.

We can all remember the golden days of our early life, when no hard-and-fast line had yet been drawn for us between the real and the impossible, and when everything was wonderful because everything was new. That was the roseate time when we knew that at the base of every rainbow there lay buried a pot of real gold. We heard fairies whispering in the thickets of the woods, and could point out the hillocks where gnomes came up each night and gamboled in the moonlight. Then all of us dreamed rare dreams and cherished harmlessly delightful fancies; for the gray old world was very beautiful, and our lives were flushed

with the light that dies away so soon. There
were no Educationists in that paradise to which
so many men and women, now grown grim and
mirthless, sometimes look back with an unwonted dimness of the eyes. But to-day appears the brisk and practical Young Person of
nineteen or thereabouts, fresh from a Training
College and with no illusions and no sympathies about her. She bursts in upon the penetralia of childhood, and knocks its household
gods to smithereens. Fairy stories? Nonsense! Giants? Bosh! With a ruthless efficiency she annihilates the gentle friends of the
child's imagination, deposes Santa Claus, mocks
at the virtues of the Wishbone, and drives with
jeers the Sand Man out of existence. Then she
gets down to work and trots out her own substitutes for all these things. The children must
begin to absorb some scraps of history; they
must draw geometrical figures instead of rings
for "migs." No more singing at their play of
the disaster that befell London Bridge, or of
the Farmer who stamps his foot and claps
his hands and turns around to view the land.
" Eeny-meeny-mony-mike" is silly gibber-
ish. " Monkey, monkey, barrel of beer" is
low. None of this for the wise young lady
who now runs things! She will teach her

flock some real instructive and improving songs, about minerals, for instance, and when she takes them out to walk she will make them peep and botanize with her in a way to give Linnæus myelitis. Then the little things, instead of playing around in God's free air and in a healthily unconscious way, are thrust into a kindergarten, where they sit and make worst-ed parallelograms on a piece of cardboard, and learn a sort of complicated drill that keeps them unnaturally alert ; while through the whole performance they are watched and egged on to emulation until their little faces flush and all their sensitive little nerves are tingling with unhealthy excitement. They learn some things ; but what they learn is valueless, while what they lose in learning it is beyond all price. At times, perhaps, some mother whose mind is troubled by these new works and ways will timidly suggest her doubts about the wisdom of it all ; but the brisk Young Person will promptly and rather patronizingly inform her that it rests upon a Psychological Basis, and that it is just what Frœbel meant. And so we see growing up about us a generation of shrill, self-conscious, and insufferably priggish brats.

This strain of thought is always started by the sight of the children's picture-books that

every year load down the counters of the book-
shops in anticipation of the holidays; for the
Educationist has not yet abolished Christmas,
probably because he requires a short vacation
himself, in which he can go off somewhere and
think. But he has done what he could by issuing a ukase (which has probably a Psychological Basis, too) as to the sort of picture-books
that children should be allowed to see. No
more of those demoralizing and quite absurd
old stories of which both text and pictures have
wrought such a havoc in the past! Why, they
can be proved to be filled with falsehood. Take
the pernicious tale called *Jack and the Bean-
stalk*. Everybody knows that beans could
never grow to such a height as this story represents, nor if they did, would human life be
possible at such an altitude. And as for the
Giant—why, it is a well-known anthropologi-
cal fact that there are no giants. See Quatre-
fages and Schwartz. Then the story goes on
to speak of a talking harp and a hen that lays
golden eggs. What glaring improbabilities!
An inanimate object like a harp cannot possibly possess phonological attributes; auto-
matic sounds of any kind would be out of the
question. And as for the hen—no treatise on
ornithology ever includes among the ova of

gallinaceous bipeds any such phenomenon. In a word, these things being easily demonstrated to be absolutely false and without any foundation in fact, will any one seriously advise that children should be allowed to hear of them? Would you have them grow up to manhood and womanhood believing in magic beans, and talking harps, and giants? The thing is pedægogically unsound and psychologically monstrous! No! if children must have anything so frivolous as a picture-book for mere amusement (a thing to be deplored), let them at least have books that may indirectly familiarize them with the world as it is, and not with unrealities like talking harps and aureous eggs. Let us through the eye give them some knowledge of zoölogical truths, and let these be depicted in a way to soothe and to tranquillize rather than to stimulate an unhealthy imagination. Finally, these picture-books in primary colors are wholly inartistic, and check the æsthetic development of a child's mind. Give us rather drawings in delicate outline and permeated by the influence of Art.

These notions have gradually been instilled into the minds of fathers and mothers, and have finally filtered through to the minds of publishers as well, so that at last one finds everywhere the sort of picture-book for which the Educationist cries out. They are roughly to be divided into two classes — the animal picture-book and the purely artistic picture-book.

The animal picture-book is not a picture-book of the old kind, in which animals are the protagonists of tragedies and comedies. There is no story in the new picture-book, but just animals—principally cows. One doesn't quite see how it is that cows are supposed to be most fitted for the contemplation of the New Child. Perhaps the calm of the cow, her unimaginative turn of mind, and her thoughtful nature make her psychologically safe; but anyhow there she is, occupying whole pages of a hundred picture-books. First you see the cow in the foreground gazing in profile over a fence; then you see the same cow in the middle distance looking around for something to eat; last you see the cow in the background with her hind legs carefully foreshortened and doing nothing in particular. *Toujours* cow. The drawing is very carefully done; the cow's *chiaroscuro* is excellent. The disposition of the tail is always carefully thought out with reference to the general scheme of composition. But the Old Child would want to know what it all meant; and when told that it had no meaning, no insidious story, he would have thought that there was just a little too much cow; and the perfection of the *chiaroscuro* would not wholly fill the void caused by the absence of meaning and of story. What the New Child thinks of it I personally do not know.

Next to the cow, the pig is greatly favored by the makers of these picture-books. Now the pig is all right. He has played an honorable and even an exciting part in the child's books of the past, from the Little Pig who went to market to the other Little Pig who built him a house out of straw against which the Wolf huffed and puffed till he blew it down; and the far more fortunate Little Pig who fooled the Wolf and finally scalded him to death in a big kettle. But the latter-day pig is not a pig of that kind. He is just a plain pig with no mind, a pig who has had no adventures, a pig about whose life there is no dark mystery, no tragedy, and no triumph—in fact, an ordinary pig with as little imagination as an Educationist.

The purely artistic picture-book is different in subject. Its style of picture is very well exemplified in the designs which that very clever artist, Miss Ethel Reed, occasionally draws for children's books. Miss Reed's designs usually show a female face sometimes looking to the right and sometimes looking to the left and sometimes looking at the reader. There is a flurry of buds and leaves and butterflies and other small *hors d'œuvres* gracefully disposed about the figure, and that is all. It is very artistic and daintily drawn; but again the Old Child would ask, "What is it all about?" And the answer would have to be that it isn't about anything. The present writer received rather a shock the other day when he spoke to a friend about this matter, and said that he thought that a child could hardly find much to interest him in such drawings as those of Miss Reed.

"Why," cried my friend, "you're entirely mistaken! My little girl is so fascinated by these pictures that she carries the book to bed with her at night!"

Here was a blow that made me gasp. No one likes to have his theories upset in this way.

"Yes," he went on, "she looks at them by the hour, and insists on my making up a story about each one."

O veritas sanctissima! Here was confirmation strong as holy writ! So the New Child is not so very different from the Old Child, after all. The Story is still the thing, and all that the Educationist has yet accomplished is to throw the burden of providing it on the parent instead of on the author!

It is in this latter fact that one descries some hope of ultimately returning sanity. When the overworked parent begins to realize that the child is going to have the story just the same as ever, he will also begin to reflect that it might just as well be told in the book as extracted from his own inexperienced fancy; that Nature is still a good deal stronger than Art; that though the Educationist may temporarily pitch her out with a psychological dung-fork, she will steal in again through the back door as irrepressible as ever; and that, granting the necessity of the Story, there will never be any stories like those fine old tales that have defied the tooth of time and will defy the dogmas even of the all-wise Educationist. Then will Jack the Giant Killer stand forth once more in his great nursery epic; and Little Red Riding Hood, whose story has all the subtle elements of a Greek drama, will come again into her own; and Blue Beard will be heard still thundering at the foot of the tower while Sister Anne waves her signal to the rescuers.

One argument against these books deserves some little serious consideration, because, on the face of it, it is not devoid of plausibility. It is asserted that the scenes of killing and wounding and battle and slaughter in which some of them abound are unduly horrifying to the sensitive mind of a child ; that they will frighten and excite and alarm, and are therefore unwholesome in their effect upon the mind and nerves. But this assertion only goes to show how little, with all his vaunted psychology, the Educationist really knows about the nature of a child's mind. He ascribes to the child, in fact, attributes that are impossible without an experience which no child can possibly possess. Thus, for example, when you tell the Educationist how Jack drew his sword and decapitated the Two Headed Giant, he, being a grown man with a knowledge of physiological facts, can conjure up the horrors of an actual killing—the gushing blood, the shriek of agony, the monstrous body swaying and falling, and the inevitableness and finality of death. But what does the child know of all this ? To it the cutting off of the head is not in itself more startling than the taking off of a hat. Of course, it is rather uncomfortable for a Giant to be without any head ; but he is a bad old Giant anyway and deserves some little annoyance of this sort for stealing the poor people's pigs and cattle. If he should repent, however, there is no reason why his head should not be clapped on again all right and be as good as new, just as when the Maid was in the Garden hanging out the Clothes and her nose was carried off by a predatory blackbird, it wasn't long before little Jenny Wren came and satisfactorily replaced it. To the child's simple faith everything is possible; it knows as little of anatomy as of antiseptic surgery; and its imagination, however active and daring, is necessarily circumscribed and conditioned by the limitations of its knowledge. Consequently, just as young David Copperfield read of Tom Jones and Humphrey Clinker and found them harmless creatures because his own mind had not yet eaten of the tree of life that gives a knowledge of good and evil, so to the child in the nursery, the combats and wild scenes of the story-book are as innocent as summer picnics.

It is perhaps permissible to think that when the present fad for over-refining the processes of children's education has been dropped, when the Psychological Basis has been laid comfortably to rest, and when we all go back to a

simpler and more natural way of looking at
these things, the child's picture-book will be
found to have been modified in only one respect by reason of this pow-wow. It is likely
that the pictures themselves, while keeping to
the old themes, or to themes that are not different in general spirit, will be more artistic in
their execution, and that is all. Then we shall
have a quite ideal picture-book—one whose
illustrations will suggest the story that lies
behind them, and at the same time will deserve respect for the adequacy of their execution.

There must be in the ideal illustrative imagination and insight, originality and felicity
of execution ; and there should also be a subtle touch of humor unobtrusively suggested—
the sort of underlying humor always present
in a child's mind when it is playing robbers,
for instance, or anything else that is purely
make-believe, and which is quite consistent
with the greatest external gravity and apparent faith in the little drama. It is, in fact, the
sub-consciousness of the fiction as a fiction, the
duality of the thought, the underlying knowledge that the play is really nothing but a
play, that so tickles a child's fancy and gives
to the whole thing its greatest zest. Hence

14

the ideal pictures for a child will always man-
age to suggest this very feeling, will make you
know that the artist is himself within the
charmed circle, that he is playing with the
children and making believe as hard as they
are ; and all the while you must be conscious
that his eyes, like theirs, have just a glint of
fun in them, just the suspicion of a twinkle
that shows how well he understands the rules
of the game. Moreover, each picture must inevitably make you feel that there is a story
behind it, and must excite in the mind of the
child who sees it a strong desire to know just
what that story is.

Let us live, therefore, in the hope that ere
long there will come to children a glorious
Renaissance of the Natural, when they will no
more be fed with formulas and made to learn
so many improving things. Childhood is short
enough at the very best ; the dreams of children vanish all too soon ; the facts of life confront them grimly even while the baby look
still lingers in their eyes ; and surely he is no
real lover of his kind who would begrudge
them this one small corner of delight and enter
in with sullen tread to mar the heaven that lies
about us in our infancy.

AMERICAN FEELING TOWARDS ENGLAND

AMERICAN FEELING TOWARDS ENGLAND

THE Venezuelan complication of a year ago quite naturally called forth a swarm of articles in the newspapers and in the magazines. In this country such published discussion was, in general, pretty closely confined to the merits of the question immediately at issue, but in England it took a much wider range, and appeared to centre very largely around the general subject of American feeling towards England, as to which the English seem of late to feel an unusual curiosity. For many weeks it was impossible to take up an English periodical without finding either an elaborate article or at least a long paragraph devoted to more or less exoteric speculation upon this rather interesting topic. The writers in every case, however, were Englishmen, and, in consequence, no very satisfactory and convincing analysis appeared; for the subject is one with which no Englishman, from the nature of the case, is competent to deal, because such knowl-

edge as Englishmen possess, or think they possess, is necessarily derived from their reading
of our newspapers or from their own very superficial acquaintance with a very limited portion of our population.   Even Mr. Goldwin
Smith, who has spent a good portion of his
life in and near the United States, cannot be
accepted as a safe guide ; for while he doubtless
knows many Americans, and has heard and
read much that is published here, he cannot
have come closely into contact with the great
mass of the American people, with whose point
of view alone this discussion has to do.   The
real feeling of a nation, especially of a nation
like our own, is not to be gleaned from the
highly - colored pronouncements of a sensa-
tional press, nor, on the other hand, from the
after-dinner chat of a tactful and hospitable en-
tertainer, who for the moment lets his personal liking for a distinguished guest inspire him
with a purely cenatory cordiality towards the
nation whom that guest for the moment typi-
fies.   Hence it is that whatever has been published in England gives only an outsider's view,
which is hostile or friendly, according to the
writer's own limited and personal observations,
and in many cases, also, according to the spirit
in which his investigation has been conducted.

Two letters, however, published in two English journals are really worth remembering. Each very fairly represents one of the two general opinions held in England of America and American sentiment, and, taken together, they may serve as a text for the consideration of a very interesting question.

The first is a letter written to the London *Times* by Dr. Conan Doyle. Dr. Doyle has lately visited the United States. He has met many Americans, both in public and in the apparently confidential intercourse of private life, and he doubtless thinks that he is very well qualified to expound the national sentiment of our people towards his own country. Dr. Doyle believes that there is a good deal of hostility towards England, though not towards Englishmen ; and he regards this feeling as a sort of tradition, an historic survival from the past, and not as anything very definite, very specific, or very reasonable. He points out that in American schools the portions of American history most carefully studied are those that treat of our two great struggles with England, and he expresses the opinion that by continually dwelling upon the events of the Revolutionary War and of the War of 1812 American youth are trained up to regard England as a sort of hereditary foe, towards whom it is both proper and patriotic to express and actually to feel a certain amount of rather vague hostility which could not, however, be justified by the facts of the present day. Dr. Doyle is good enough himself to speak with much friendliness of the American people, and to express his belief that such bitterness as survives from the past will die away as the two nations grow more and more to realize their community of interest, and to know each other better. In short, his view is that of the modern Liberal— well meaning, anxious to be just and fair, and fully convinced that he is perfectly familiar with all sides of a by no means complicated question.

The other letter appeared in the *Saturday Review* and bore the signature of Mr. Morley Roberts, a rather obscure young English writer. This document is considerably shorter than Dr. Doyle's and far more snappy in its diction. It was called forth primarily by the appeal of the English authors to their American brethren—an appeal which Mr. Roberts very indignantly repudiates. Having done this, he goes on to set forth some notions of his own. He regards Americans as distinctly and bitterly hostile to England and to Englishmen. He asserts that we are "rancorous," and he very frankly says that this feeling is most heartily reciprocated in England. The concluding paragraphs of his letter deserve to be quoted in full :

" No Englishman with imperial instincts can look with anything but contempt on the Monroe Doctrine. The English, and not the inhabitants of the United States, are the greatest power in the two Americas; and no dog of a Republic can open its mouth to bark without our good leave. Personally, I look forward to a time when a social and political revolt shall tear the heterogeneous plutocratic fabric of the States to fragments, and then the more truly democratic England may come by her heritage.

" Those who sign this precious paper go on to say that we are proud of the United States. Sir, we *might* be proud of them; but to say that we *are* proud of them is to speak most disingenuously. Who can be proud of a politically corrupt and financially rotten country, with no more than a poor minority vainly striving for health ? . . .

" If literature is the only bond between us and this most ill-mannered country, it may be time for us to repudiate American copyright before the Americans repudiate it. But literature is no real bond, because not one American in a thousand—no, not one in ten thousand—has had his manners made less brutal by the most casual acquaintance with it. For these reasons I wish to dissociate myself from an appeal to any country, and more particularly to the United States."

Mr. Roberts's delightfully frank and evidently honest letter represents the deliberate opinion of the High Tory, and one that is held in its extreme form by many Englishmen who are not Tories. In a less degree, I think, it is held also by a majority, if not of all Englishmen, at least of all the Englishmen who count.

Both the views expressed in these letters are clearly wrong—Dr. Doyle's because it mistakes both the cause and the direction of such unfriendly sentiment towards England as exists in the United States; and Mr. Roberts's, because it so immensely exaggerates the extent and nature of that sentiment. It is not true, as Dr. Doyle thinks, that Americans still cherish any feeling that was an inheritance from our early struggles with England. What he says would have seemed reasonable in the forties, when, as Mr. Howells has narrated in his *Boy's Town*, the American school-boy was taught to regard the "Bridish" as a bloodthirsty and relentless foe, to be classed with the devil and all his works. There were many men then living who had a keen personal recollection of the massacres at Tappan and in the Wyoming Valley, who had themselves experienced the loathsome horrors of the Eng-

lish prison-ships, or had later seen the nation's
Capitol in flames. But that generation has
now passed away, and with them the reality
of these experiences. Americans are not much
given to living in the past; and if they now
recall the memory of these two wars, it is because they regard them as picturesque episodes in our national history, and not at all
because the recollection feeds fat an ancient
grudge. In fact, we can all now contemplate
the records of 1776 and 1812 with a good deal
of complacency; for in the first war the colonies distinctly triumphed over the mother
country, while the second conflict ended in
the tacit abandonment by England of the
right of search whose enforcement had brought
about the struggle.

It is a pity, then, that no adequate expression of American feeling towards England has
yet been written down by an American, because such an utterance would greatly enlight-
en the English mind in its present condition
of uncertainty, and would be valuable also as
a corrective to much of the loose talk that is
heard in this country on the political stump
and in the columns of the political newspaper.

What is the real feeling that Americans entertain towards England? And when we say Americans, we do not, on the one hand, mean the politicians, who are mere reeds shaken by the wind, and who study the popular feeling so intently as to lose all sense of perspective, and therefore fail to see the wood by reason of the trees. Nor do we mean those persons who are Americans by act of the courts rather than by right of birth—Americans upon whose papers of naturalization the ink is scarcely dry, and in whom still smoulders the memory of Old World feuds. And, on the other hand, one does not mean those despicable curs of native birth, who may be heard from time to time yelping at their country in foreign clubs and the smoking-rooms of transatlantic steamers, and who are thrilled with delight down to the very depths of their infinitesimal little souls when some fatuous foreigner tells them that he "really would never have taken them to be Americans!" We mean, rather, that great silent mass of our countrymen whose nationality is inherited from many generations of Anglo - Saxon ancestors, and who have learned their Americanism at their father's fireside and not from the scare - heads of a newspaper—men who have no political ambitions up their sleeve, and who do not rush into print, but who stand for sobriety and sense, and whose matured opinion, in the long run, makes and unmakes Presidents and Senates, and bends the government's whole policy to its silent will. How do these men feel towards England, the home of their race and the source of the great stream of our national traditions?

It is told of Charles Dickens, that on his second visit to this country he fell into conversation with an American upon this very subject; and finally, with that peculiar sort of tact which so many Englishmen possess, he remarked:

"Oh, as far as we are concerned, it's perfectly simple, you know. We all of us love Americans, but we hate America."

To which the American is said to have replied, rather slowly:

"Well, with us it's just the other way: we all of us love England—but we hate Englishmen."

There is a great deal of truth packed away in this sentence, though it needs a certain amount of exegetical commentary which is perhaps most easily conveyed in an allegorical form. The English nation is a good deal like the elder brother in the regulation British novel, who in due time, by right of primogeniture, succeeds to the ancestral estates and the family mansion. We Americans, on the other hand, represent the younger brother who inherits nothing, and who if he remains at home must do so as the mere dependent of the heir. The old home is very dear to him. It has always been his home as truly as his brother's. He knows every nook and corner of the park, every tree in the woodlands, every leaf of the lustrous ivy on the towers. To leave it all is inexpressibly hard. Yet he is not of a stock that takes kindly to dependence; and so at last he tears himself away with a hearty goodbye to his brother, and the suspicion of a tear in his eye for the old days that are over; and going out into a new land in a new world, he begins the fight for fortune. He battles with the forces of nature, and overcomes them; he subdues the forest, the wild beast, and the savage, and makes a new home for himself by his indomitable energy and courage and perseverance. Years go on, and at last he hews out a fortune also. Everything prospers, and he grows richer and richer, until finally his wildest dreams are realized; and then his first thought is once more to visit the home of his childhood. He crosses the sea, a man strong and successful, one who has lived the large, free life of the

New World, and he hurries along over the well-known roads with a heart full of generous emotion, dreaming in his simplicity of a royal welcome from the brother whom he left behind so long ago, and towards whom his very soul goes out in his love for home and kindred. And when at last he rushes into his presence with all this pent-up enthusiasm ready to overflow, and with the breezy breath of a thousand leagues of sea about him, he finds the brother whom he had so longed for, a stiff, smug, decorous, and frigid person, who looks him over a little curiously, who gives him a couple of fingers to shake, and who asks him in rather a languid way whether he is going to stay all night! The enthusiasm is killed in an instant; and when he finds that his elder regards him with a certain supercilious disdain, as one who has evidently lost, in the outlandish countries where he has lived, all traces of his early breeding—one whose very success has made him a little vulgar—then perhaps the younger brother swears a little to himself, and would rather like to punch the other's head. But he never quite forgets the tie between them, and if his elder were in need, or if some stranger were to attack him, all these private grievances would be put away in an instant, and he would stand by the head of his house with both purse and power to the very last extremity.

And this is about the way it is with the American. He loves England with a fervor and a passion of which no Englishman has any conception. It means to his consciousness far more than it can mean to any Englishman. When he visits it his whole heart leaps at the first sight of the poppy-sprinkled meadows and the ivied walls of its sleepy old towns. It is his home; its history is his history; its glory is his glory too. But the people—that is another matter. It is not the memory of old-time wars that affects him. For these he cares no more than for the First Crusade. No Anglo-Saxon ever bears malice towards a former opponent in a good, square, stand-up fight. But when he finds his kindred in the old home looking at him with a sort of tolerant contempt, when he notes the ostentatious condescension of their manner, and the absurd assumption of superiority that is theirs, then he begins to think of things that happened in his own recollection; and when he does so think of them he waxes hot. He recalls how in the darkest period of our Civil War the English statesmen who had once posed as the friends of the United States greeted the news of our

disasters with mingled cheers and sneers; how
they set their names to the list of those who
pledged great sums of money to the support
of our opponents; how amid bland assurances
of ignorance they let slip from English ports
the privateers that swept our vessels from the
sea; how, when English ships were anchored
beside our ships of war in neutral harbors their
crews made night hideous with their insulting
songs and cheers for the national enemy; how
a great noble like Lord Hartington ostenta-
tiously displayed a Confederate emblem at a
gathering in New York, where he had been
welcomed as a guest; how in a thousand ways
the representatives of England gloated over
our misfortunes and mocked at our successes.
And if the American be a Southerner his feeling is not very different, for he knows now
what he did not at the time so clearly see:
that English sympathy with the South was
wholly selfish and self-seeking; that it waned
and died when the cause of the Confederacy
grew hopeless; and that its only source was
the desire to discredit and destroy the great
Republic whose existence was a perpetual reproach to the pig-headed folly of an English
king.

Yet it is probably not these public acts of

15

avowed ill-wishers that have most irritated
American sentiment against Englishmen; it
is rather the half-unconscious, blundering way
in which the average Briton contrives, even in
his clumsy attempts at civility, to reveal a
mental attitude that reflects dislike and differ-
entiation—an attitude which puts Americans
into the place of " poor relations " to be asked,
so to speak, to warmed-over dinners and the
hashed mutton of courtesy; or that prompts
him, when he visits this side of the Atlantic,
to appear at an evening reception in a tweed
suit.   An anecdote told by General Badeau of
President Grant's visit to England will illustrate our meaning:

"At one manufacturing town he (General Grant)
stayed at a house where every honor was paid him
and every courtesy extended. But his hosts took
him to visit the steward of a lord who lived near by.
He was permitted to see the state apartments in the
absence of his lordship, and he lunched in the land-
steward's room and not in the earl's. The steward
was probably an abler and better educated man than
his master, and General Grant was too good a democrat not to appreciate this fact and to respect his
host; but if he had been an English nobleman neither
steward nor manufacturer would have dreamed of
entertaining him."

This was a trifling incident in itself, but it is

beautifully illustrative of the way in which the Englishman turns even his hospitality into a discourtesy by making it accentuate the low esteem in which he holds his guest.

There are times when even the most unemotional American who calls to mind such things as these, and who reads perhaps some bit of coarse abuse like that of Mr. Morley Roberts—there are times, I say, when he would exult in shouldering a rifle for a march over the Canadian frontier, and when he would see with joy the humiliation of England at the hand of the United States. Yet there never has come a time when he would wish to see that humiliation inflicted by any other hands. He would perhaps welcome a struggle, but it must be, so to speak, a purely family affair for the clearing up of scores that affect no other people—an affair to be settled by a fine piece of give-and-take fighting, with no ill-feeling as an aftermath. Whenever a foreign power attempts to put an affront on England, as the insolent young cub of a German Kaiser lately tried to do, the American feels as though he, too, had received a slap full in the face. And then, when the news is flashed across the sea that his English kinsmen have risen to resent the insult, united and unflinching in the face

of danger; when he hears that fleets are mo-
bilized and that troops are rallying to their
colors with the splendid efficiency that is the
attribute of England in the hour of danger,
then his whole heart goes out to them in a
thrill of sympathy, and, putting aside the recollection of his former grievances, he would
rather like to take a shot on his own account
at the enemy whom, for the time being, he
regards as an enemy of the entire race.

This, I think, is a fair expression of American sentiment towards England — a curious
mingling of pride in the ancestral home with
a very real dislike for much that Englishmen
have done and are still doing.   And this view
of the case is one to be commended to the very
careful consideration of the English ; for it rests
with them to say which of these two feelings
shall in the end dominate and at last obliter-
ate the other.   Should they go on exercising
their peculiar gift of making enemies, the hour
for repentance may come and come too late.
Some day, perhaps, when the meteor flag shall
have been dimmed for the first time by the
shadow of a great defeat, when the Battle of
Dorking shall have been actually fought, and
when the spiked helmets are swarming over
the downs of Surrey in irresistible conver-

gence upon undefended London, even the most self-satisfied Englishmen may regret that of their own deliberate choice they killed in the hearts of the American people a feeling which to-day still lives, and which tells us that the prosperity and the greatness and the honor of England are in no small degree our own inheritance.

PRESIDENT CLEVELAND

PRESIDENT CLEVELAND

WITH his retirement from the supreme executive office Mr. Cleveland's public life may be regarded as definitely ended. Our traditional and quite indefensible system, which gives no official rank to an ex-President, and therefore deprives the nation of the exceptional experience and the exceptionally impartial counsel of him who has passed through the great ordeal of administering the mightiest popular government known to the modern world, imposes upon Mr. Cleveland, as upon his predecessors, the dignified yet unfruitful obscurity of private station; for with scarcely an exception, our American Presidents have felt that they owed it to the majesty of the office that was once their own, to listen to no ordinary call of public service, and to hold aloof from all the din and uproar of party strife. In consequence, Mr. Cleveland already belongs to history; and even now the attempt is being made to assign to him and to his ad-

ministration their proper place in the annals of
the American Republic.

That such an attempt is absurdly premature
is so obvious as to need no argument. With
the passion of partisanship still strong in the
minds alike of those who fought against him
and of those who battled with him, the sense
of true historical perspective cannot possibly
exist to-day; and with the echoes of a great
political battle still reverberating in the ear,
no one can hear as yet the calm, clear voice
that ultimately stills all others as it pronounces
the final verdict of a nation's history.

But though it is too soon to weigh the policies and to judge the measures that are now
inseparably linked with the story of Mr. Cleveland's public life, or to pretend to know how
beneficial or how harmful is to be their influence upon the political welfare of the American people, it is, nevertheless, perhaps by no
means an impossible task for one outside the
range of purely partisan activity to form some
sort of tentative opinion of the man himself as
an administrator and as a party leader; for,
putting aside the merits of the ends that he
has aimed to reach, the manner in which he
has pursued them is wholly a matter of recorded fact, and in no respect a matter of

opinion; and it surely may even now be viewed with reasonable impartiality as a very interesting political and personal study.

For some cause or other, Americans have always found a peculiar pleasure in dwelling upon the striking contrasts that are so abundant in the lives of their public men. To recall in the presence of a stately Senator the fact that he was once a bobbin-boy ; to see in the victorious general a whilom tanner or grocer's clerk ; and to look back of the President seated in the simple chair that serves him as a very real throne from which to direct the destinies of seventy millions of people, and remember the rail-splitter or canal-boatman of twenty or thirty years ago, seems to titillate agreeably a certain almost universal instinct. Perhaps this feeling is a part of the national irreverence ; or perhaps it is only a manifestation of the national sense of humor which finds an especial piquancy in vivid contrasts ; or perhaps again, at bottom, it rests in some subtle way upon an intensely American admiration for the nerve, the capacity, and the "gumption" that enable some men to fight their way up from obscurity against tremendous odds and to wrest a brilliant success from the reluctant hand of Destiny. However this may be, the career of Mr. Cleveland is perhaps more full of startling contrasts, of striking anomalies, and of unexpected paradoxes, than can be found in the history of any other of our Presidents. No American in public life has ever experienced more rapid and astonishing turns of fortune; no man has raised and faced and fought so many deep-rooted political and personal prejudices; no man has broken through so many thoroughly established political traditions.

Of all our American Presidents there are four who stand out conspicuously above the rest as representing four distinct types, each very characteristic and very national, and each differing essentially from the other three. In Washington we see the highest type of the colonial American, developed wholly under the influence of English traditions. Washington is, in fact, in his tone and temper, his point of view and his ideals, the representative upon American soil of the English gentleman and statesman, though with a difference that makes him *au fond* entirely American; and his immediate successors in the Presidency did not very far depart from the standards that were his. Even Jefferson, with all his radicalism, must be grouped in the same class, for, as is

the case with most Americans, his radicalism,
startling as it seemed to the Federalists of his
time, was only superficial ; and when one thinks
of him as strolling through the stately halls
of Monticello, a landed proprietor, his cellars
stored with rare old wines, his library filled
with the choicest books, patronizing the arts
and sciences, and having his wants supplied
by a retinue of slaves, he is readily seen to
have been the true patrician whose democracy
was in large part an intellectual assumption,
just as the political theories of the great Whig
dukes in England are found, upon analysis, to
differ in no fundamental point from the conservatism of the Tory magnates. Jackson was the
first New Man to arise in our government's history ; and he represents the rough frontiersman,
the fighter, the man who faced both nature and
the savage in a successful battle for the mastery
of the West. His election marks an epoch in our
history, a break in the traditions that bound us
closely to English influence ; and he is the first
of the American Presidents to stand firmly
and almost fiercely upon the rock of national
individuality.   Lincoln, again, is still another
type — the type of the Western provincial, a
later growth than the frontiersman, with some
of the frontiersman's traits, but more subtle,

more open to new influences, more closely in
touch with the resources of an older civilization, much more a man of thought and somewhat less a man of action.

Mr. Cleveland, when he first became known
to the nation at the time of his candidacy for
the governorship of New York in 1882, typified
a fourth and a still different kind of personality.
In him was seen the modern American who
lives in cities and represents a stratum of the
population that is every year becoming more
and more numerous with the increase of the
urban element.   He was a type of the practical,
every-day, usual citizen of moderate means and
no very marked ambitions — a blend of the
business man and the small professional person, one who knocks about with his fellows in
a give-and-take sort of way, blunt, hard-headed,
having a good digestion and a brusque, unimaginative readiness to take a hand in whatever
is going on.   His education was of the sim-
plest, his general information and reading presumably of the scantiest, and his interest in
life was pretty nearly bounded by the limits
of the city of Buffalo.   As a practising lawyer
he appeared in the local courts, and, though
well thought of by his fellow-lawyers, and
though at times intrusted with the conduct

of cases of considerable importance, he was
not known beyond the local circuit. A bachelor, he had no need of a large income. His
spare time was spent with cronies of his own
kind. His recreation was derived largely from
the intricacies of the game of pinochle, played
in the comfortable back room of a beer-garden;
and perhaps this circumstance is in itself enough
to give a fair idea of his general environment.
When the eventful convention was held that
nominated him for the governorship, Mr. Cleveland took charge of his own canvass in person,
sitting all through the sultry summer day in
a small bedroom of his hotel, with a tub of
cracked ice and innumerable bottles beside
him, conferring with his cronies, receiving visits from country delegates, and by a sort of
professional joviality bidding for the favor of
that interesting class of politicians whom his
chief advocate in recent years has generically
described as Boys.

Elected Governor by an unprecedented majority, owing to bitter dissensions in the opposing party, Mr. Cleveland entered upon a wider
field and one that must have seemed at first a
post of limitless exactions. But his lack of
imagination stood him in good stead. He bent
his back to the load and did each day's work

as it came. Unused to large responsibilities, unable as yet to discriminate between the duties that are executive and the duties that are purely clerical, and retaining all the fussiness of the provincial business man, he viewed all questions as equally important, attending personally to all his correspondence, insisting upon examining for himself every item and detail of the executive routine, and giving hours of his time each day to the minutiæ that the merest clerk could have attended to with quite as much efficiency. But this was, after all, a manifestation of the conscientiousness that showed itself far more commendably in higher matters. The rough, blunt independence of the man and his unimaginative turn of mind made him indifferent to the insidious influences that rise like a malarial mist about the possessor of high political office. Mere subtleties of suggestion were lost on this brusque Buffalonian, and anything more pointed than suggestion roused in him a sort of cross-grained spirit of opposition that brooked no guidance. Suave, astute, and wily leaders of the party, like Mr. Tilden, who had expected to find the inexperienced country politician a ready instrument in their hands, were aghast to see him forging along in his own way with a sort of bull-necked stubbornness, clumsy and lumbering, yet with a power and energy which they had to recognize as very real. And the great body of the people, whose love for political independence is all the more intense because of the infrequency with which they ever have a chance to see it, applauded this burly, obstinate, tactless, but intensely earnest man. They laughed when the professional politicians were trampled on; and even the representatives of "labor," whom Mr. Cleveland calmly defied by his veto of a well-known bill, at heart respected him for his courage and his honesty.

Then came Mr. Cleveland's nomination to the Presidency, followed by the memorable campaign of 1884—that shameful contest in which personal scandal was belched forth by the writers and speakers of both parties, in which foul innuendo and filthy suggestion took the place of argument, and in which clergymen vied with the shouters of the stump in spreading abroad indecent charges, while even the graves of the dead were ransacked in search of fresh material for prurient pasquinades. Mr. Cleveland was still a bachelor, and the *condottieri* of the enemy thought him a fair target for every missile. It was the most extraordinary struggle that American political history

16

has ever seen—a wild debauch of slander, and
one of which every decent citizen, Republican
or Democrat, was afterwards ashamed ; so that
by a sort of tacit consent all subsequent cam-
paigns have been fought out on purely public
issues. Mr. Cleveland stood firm under the
assaults upon his private character, though
tempted into the writing of one very indiscreet and even foolish letter; and his general
attitude was quite consistent with his reputation for frankness and sincerity. His terse
telegram to a friend at the beginning of the
onslaught furnished his partisans with a new
slogan; so that "Tell the truth" became as
popular a cry as "Burn this letter," though, as
some one rather cynically remarked at the
time, "neither was the letter burned nor was
the truth all told."

The hopeless break in the Republican party
caused by the nomination of Mr. Blaine, and
the undoubted disloyalty to him of the Conkling faction in New York, gave the Presidency
to Mr. Cleveland by a plurality of only a few
hundred votes in a single State. The record
of the past twelve years must still be fresh in
the minds of even the youngest of our readers.
Into the details of this eventful period we cannot go, but they are surely among the most

curious of any that our history affords. How
this untrained, unlettered, provincial lawyer,
this local politician, this heavy-handed, tactless, gruff Buffalonian drew to himself as his
own personal following the most refined and
highly-trained and finical men of the party
that had always hated the very name of Democrat; how even those, like Mr. Lowell, who
still remained his nominal opponents, spoke
of his sincerity and single-mindedness with
something like the fervor of enthusiasm; and
how he made his own those views of government and economic policy that had long been
viewed as suited only to the theorist and the
doctrinaire; how he imposed them upon his
own reluctant party, and for the first time in
many decades saved it from a purely defensive
attitude in the arena of national politics; how,
though defeated for re-election, he was a third
time nominated and then triumphantly elected
over his formerly successful rival; how he came
into power again with a united party and a
great legislative majority behind him; how in
a few short months he found himself without
a loyal following; how he was finally com-
pelled to give at least a moral support to the
very man who represented the idea most
thoroughly antagonistic to that with which

his own career is closely linked; and how he
at last went forth from office into private life
after having been repudiated by his own party,
which he left disorganized and divided—these
are but a few of the many strange anomalies
which the record of his administration presents.
Yet even in his less important acts an equal
amount of contradiction is apparent.   That
the man who in 1888 denounced the baleful
influence of capital should end by standing
forth as the chosen champion of capital; that
the President whose first official utterance proclaimed the unwisdom of a second term of
office should himself become three times a can-
didate; that the politician who uttered words
of comfort to the Homestead rioters should
have stretched the Presidential prerogative almost to the point of breaking in order to quell
by military force an outbreak quite identical
in origin; that the strenuous advocate of an
improved civil service should ever have put
the machinery of appointment at the disposal
of Mr. Eugene Higgins and Mr. Logan Car-
lisle; and that the statesman whose alleged
subserviency to England was for years a gibe
with all his enemies should have hurled against
Great Britain the most warlike message penned
by any American President since the time of

Polk—all these things in their way are just as remarkable and just as paradoxical as any of the greater incidents of his career.

In forming an estimate of the place in history which Mr. Cleveland and his administration will ultimately occupy, a sharp distinction will have to be made between that side of him which is purely personal and that which belongs to the sphere of statesmanship. This distinction is one that has in general been overlooked in all the recently published analyses of his public services. It is, for example, impossible to deny that he has made a strong and ineffaceable impression upon the mind of the American people. It is equally impossible to deny that he has exemplified some of the most admirable traits that are demanded of the governing man; that he has been fearless, independent, honest, and sincere; that never for a moment has he bent his neck to the collar of a "boss"; that very seldom has he allowed any consideration of his own personal interest to move him; that he has been master of his official household in a sense that has been rarely true of any American Executive; that he and he alone, for good or for evil, has hewn out those results that must stand for all time as landmarks in the past twelve years of

American history. He has shown himself to
be, as a man, one of the most distinctly individual characters of the time; and to him as
to a President whose influence has been strongly felt, a place among the foremost must be
given.

It is only when one comes to view his work
as a statesman that opinions will very seriously differ; and until the present generation shall
have passed away all such opinions will be utterly antipodal and quite irreconcilable. A public man may be all that Mr. Cleveland's warmest
friends have claimed for him—vigorous, upright,
forceful, and single-minded—and yet fall short
of statesmanship. For a statesman, like a soldier
and like an orator, must be finally and unspar-
ingly judged solely by the measure of his success; and this is especially true of one who
fills the responsible office of the American
Executive. The function of the President
under our system is most intensely practical.
Vested with immense, and in many things
with a more than monarchical power, answer-
able within the limits of his prerogative to no
one, and knowing that prerogative to be not
very accurately defined, armed with the thun-
derbolt of the veto power, having unlimited
patronage at his command, and secure in the

tenure of his office for a period that cannot be abridged, the responsibility which rests upon him is correspondingly tremendous. He is at once the head of the State and the head of a party ; and both the welfare of the State and the welfare of the party are committed to his single keeping. Before his election he has subscribed to a definite programme of national policy representing the matured convictions of his own judgment. He has adopted a political creed that is accepted by him and by the party whose leadership he holds as embodying the immediate necessities of the nation. And therefore, when elected, he is bound by every obligation of honor and of conscience to embody these same views and principles in the national legislation and administration.

Hence, the American President is not placed in office primarily to illustrate the higher ethical virtues, but to *do* things ; so that his success or his failure depends almost entirely upon the manner in which these objects are accomplished. And in the discharge of the task, the true statesman will adapt his methods to the attainment of his ends, having a due regard to proportion, not exalting petty measures into the place of vital issues, nor enshrining whims and glorifying ephemeral fads, but keeping the

greater purpose steadily in view, and subordi-
nating questions of detail and of temporary
moment to the solemn pledges that he has
given to the people. And in doing this he
must work with such instruments as he has at
hand and use to the full the powers that have
been committed to his care. In the face of a
great national emergency, he will not ultimately suffer in the estimation of the people
if he even decline to look too closely at ab-
stract theories of duty, or if he be not over nice
in his use of the means at his disposal. This,
to be sure, to the political purists, is something
worse than heresy; but it is justified by the
whole history of modern government: for had
Elizabeth and Burleigh and Walsingham been
political purists, England in the sixteenth century would have been overwhelmed by the
Continental coalitions; had Cavour been a
political purist, United Italy would have still
remained the unsubstantial dream of a few
poor visionaries; had Bismarck been a political purist, the German Empire would have
slumbered for another century in the cave of
Barbarossa. It is, no doubt, a hard saying
that in the statesman, purity of motive, integrity of purpose, and the courage of conviction are not enough to confer enduring fame;

yet this is emphatically true : and history shows that merely negative results and excellent intentions can give no rank comparable with that which he attains who with wisdom, calmness, and the higher strength which does not bluster, conquers a complete success and leaves a mark upon the record of supreme achievement.

Judged, then, by such a test as this, it is very hard to see how Mr. Cleveland can ever find a place in the foremost line of American statesmen. It was, indeed, unfortunate for him that practically his whole preparation for the task of governing came to him in two short years while holding the chief executive office of the State of New York. For with his naturally arbitrary and self-sufficient temperament, this formed the worst possible sort of preparation for the presidency. In the first place, the Governor of New York, in his relation to the Legislature of the State, is more influential and more irresponsible than is the President of the United States in his relation to the national Congress. And the cause of this is obvious. The New York Legislature, like all our State assemblies of the sort, is composed chiefly of men who make no claim to national distinction, and whose ambitions are very limit-

ed and local. The public does not watch them
as individuals. They make no figure in the popular mind. Consequently, their only thought
is of the petty districts which they are supposed to represent, of the voters in their immediate vicinity, and of the interests of the
section from which they come. Their activi-
ties are limited to getting through small bits
of special legislation or to engineering a dicker
with the representatives of opposing interests.
To these men the Governor is politically om-
nipotent, for the loss of his favor means the
hopeless blocking of their schemes. If, therefore, he is disposed to be arbitrary, self-sufficient, and impatient of advice, this is seldom
resented, and there is really no appreciable
check upon such tendencies, provided, as is
frequently the case, his own party control
the Legislature ; and even if he be not already
given to playing the dictator, the practical supremacy which he here enjoys will very likely
make him so. It was in this office that Mr.
Cleveland acquired such knowledge of administration on a large scale as he gained prior to
his assumption of the presidential chair ; and it
was, we say, distinctly unfortunate that his
experience should have been limited to this
one sphere, in which all his natural prone-

ness to arrogance was fostered and intensified.

The downright aggressive and unconcilia-
tory methods that he had made his own while
Governor he carried with him to the national capital; and it may be assumed that they
were in no wise modified by his consciousness
of the extraordinary fortune that had made
him the first Democratic President to be actually seated after the failures and mistakes of a
quarter of a century. He doubtless felt that if
disregard of personal and party ties, absolute
reliance upon his own judgment, intolerance
of the most friendly counsel, and an ill-sup-
pressed contempt for the experience of his
associates and followers could make him a
successful Governor and lead him directly to
the presidential chair, those same qualities
were a good enough equipment for governing
the nation.

And it was here that he made a great,
and in some respects a fatal, mistake; for the
conditions of government at Albany and at
Washington are not the same; since Congress
is a very different body in tone and in temper
from the Legislature of a State. It is just
now the fashion to decry the capacity and the
character of the men who represent their States

in the Senate and the House, to profess to
see in them only a collection of demagogues
and log-rollers and "cranks"; but to bring
against them so sweeping an indictment as this
is in reality to attack the whole system under
which the American people live.   If a free, intelligent, and keen-sighted electorate does not
or cannot choose for itself legislators who
truly represent it, then, after more than a century of trial, republican government is proved
to be a failure and its fundamental theory a
falsehood and a sham.   But as a matter of fact,
while there are doubtless in both Houses of
Congress men whose characters are soiled, men
whose aims are sordid, men whose capacity is
limited, and men whose views of the public
service are perverted and even base, it is pre-
posterous to assert that the great majority of
them are anything but patriotic, conscientious,
and sincere.   Unlike the members of a local
legislature, they are men who know that what
they do is done in the public eye.   They cherish a laudable ambition for future advance-
ment.   They have opinions of their own, and
they feel the influence of other motives than
those which actuate the obscure political eph-
emeridæ who flit across the scene at Albany,
or Madison, or Little Rock.   In their own

States they are men of standing and importance, and in the white light that beats upon
the Capitol they are not to be led by the nose
with a hook or lashed into a supine submission
even when it is a President of their own party
who cracks the whip. Hence, when Mr. Cleveland resumed at Washington the rôle that he
had played so easily at Albany, he aroused at
once in the minds even of his own partisans a
very natural resentment which deepened with
time into a feeling of the intensest personal
dislike. His capacity for making unnecessary
enemies is, indeed, one of the very strangest
facts of his career; and it has proved fatal to
the success of the two great policies that
through both his terms of office have been
the nearest to his heart. During his first administration, to be sure, while the Senate was
still in the hands of his opponents, while the
country had not even yet given an emphatic
" mandate" to the Democratic Party, and while
a return to power was still a novel and agreeable sensation, such dislike as was excited in
that party by Mr. Cleveland's tactlessness
found no loud public utterance. But when his
second term began with both Houses of Congress safely Democratic, and with an immense
popular majority behind them, the discontent

that had been slumbering so long broke forth in open opposition.

In a very able and almost convincing analysis of Mr. Cleveland's public life that has been lately published, and that is probably the work of Mr. E. L. Godkin, a practical admission of Mr. Cleveland's lack of tact is made; but it is asserted that, in the emergencies which confronted him, tact was not the quality most requisite; that stubborn courage was the one thing needful.   In consequence, the case for Mr. Cleveland is made to rest upon the negative successes that he achieved in blocking measures which he held to be unwise.   "Such work," says Mr. Godkin, "cannot be done by means of tact."   Yet on the same page of the same issue of the journal in which this argument appears Mr. Godkin denounces the expiring Congress for the purely negative character of its work; and again and again has he dwelt upon the delight experienced by Senators and Representatives alike in defeating any measure that was known to have President Cleveland's personal approval. Why, then, were these things so, and of what, when taken together, are they significant?

In Mr. Cleveland's public career two great measures of national policy stand out as those

which he has always strongly pressed and with
which his name is most distinctively associated.
The first of these was a radical reform of the
tariff upon a non-protective basis; and the second was such a modification of our financial
system as would make that system unmistak-
ably a system of gold monometallism. The
reform of the tariff seemed to him so vital an
issue that for its sake he incurred defeat at
the polls in 1888; and his party frankly accepted his views and brought him back to
office by a vast majority in 1892, after a campaign fought out upon this issue. His financial policy, which was thoroughly understood
in this campaign, was also tacitly approved by
his followers, for they nominated him with a
full knowledge of his views and of his future
action. Now, if his statesmanship is to be
judged by anything at all, it surely may be
judged by the manner in which he led his
party in relation to these two vitally important measures. And what does the record
show? With regard to the tariff, it shows that
on coming into power after a successful contest decided on this very issue, with all the
prestige that attends a party leader who has
triumphed over political traditions, with a
party pledged in its official utterances to the

policy of its chief, and with a great majority in Congress elected to carry out this pledge, the only result that was attained, after months of labor and debate, was a legislative measure so ludicrously unlike what had been promised, so inconsistent in its provisions, and so emasculated in principle, that Mr. Cleveland himself was ashamed to sign it, and allowed it to become a law without his signature. In the sphere of finance the story of his leadership is still more lamentable, for not only was no definite financial measure passed, but in the effort to accomplish something, the friction between the President and his party went beyond the stage of quiet opposition and blazed out into open revolt, so that the party itself was split into opposing factions until the majority, in absolute defiance of its chief, broke away from his leadership altogether, repudiated all his tenets, and in the Chicago Convention wrote a declaration of principles every line of which was like a slap full in the face of the President whom those same men had once triumphantly elected. Then we have the strange spectacle of Mr. Cleveland, in order to save his financial doctrines from the general wreck, throwing over all his economic theories and aiding, at least by indirection, the fortunes of Mr. McKinley, his party's foe, a man whose name is linked with the most extreme of all the tariff legislation that Mr. Cleveland had for years denounced as robbery. If this be statesmanship, then statesmanship is but a synonym for anarchy.

The partisans of Mr. Cleveland have seen fit to throw the whole responsibility of this fiasco upon the Congress that thwarted and rejected his two policies. They say that in the face of such corruption, incompetence, ignorance, and personal malice as they think existed in both Houses, no President could have done what Mr. Cleveland tried to do. They say that this very opposition is only one more tribute to his political purity and uncompromising integrity of character. They "love him for the enemies that he has made," and describe his failure by the honorific name of "success in defeat." How, they ask, could he possibly prevail in the face of such a Congress? But this question is in reality an impeachment of his statesmanship. A great party leader must do his work with such instruments as he has at hand. A Congress gathered from all sections of the country will always represent conflicting interests, and it will always be filled with men discordant in their views and diffi-

17

cult of management. But every one knows
this. This is the condition of the problem,
the premise of party government, the accepted
rule of the great political game. The mere
politician will often shrink from the task, but
the inspired statesman will master the difficulties, adapt his methods to his instruments,
prevail by management, by tact, by judicious
compromise, and in the end attain a lasting
and complete success. When a party leader,
after assuming the guidance of a great majority, and with all the power of the executive
office at his disposal, dismembers his party,
wrecks his own most cherished measures, and
then cries out that he is not responsible, owing
to the machinations of evil and malicious men,
this is to plead the baby-act in its most pre-
posterous form. And this is just where Mr.
Cleveland's lack of tact assumes a critical importance. To go bellowing and snorting
through the labyrinth of legislation like a political Minotaur, goring recklessly at every
prejudice, butting into every possible obstacle,
and trampling defiantly on every personal and
political susceptibility, is perhaps courageous,
picturesque, exhilarating, amusing, magnificent, anything else you please—but it is not
statesmanship. When Mr. Cleveland's friends

disclose the list of Senators and Representatives who severed even their personal relations with him, and who rejoiced to hamper and defeat even those measures to which they were themselves by no means hostile, merely because in so defeating them they were defeating him, is not this in reality the strongest possible indictment of his administrative capacity? Is not the possession of a temperament that rouses incessant opposition and dislike as fatal a defect in a statesman as would be the possession of a club-foot in a professional athlete? As a matter of fact, the American President has infinite resources of conciliation if he but know how to use them: social influences, the prestige of his office, and, under our system, the enormous patronage whose use in winning congressional support is sanctioned by long custom. Mr. Cleveland himself is generally held to have employed this latter instrument in the contest which resulted in the repeal of the Sherman Silver Act; and in any case, the thought of its employment need not have excited any thrills of horror in a President who nominated Mr. James J. Van Alen to the Italian mission as a reward for pecuniary contributions to a campaign fund.

It is not likely that any one to-day will claim

that in political courage, personal honor, and high appreciation of public duty, President Lincoln was inferior to Mr. Cleveland; yet to recall the history of his administration is to recall that higher type of statesmanship which succeeds, as distinct from the spurious variety which fails. The problem of government as it confronted Mr. Lincoln was far more difficult than that which Mr. Cleveland had to meet. Elected by only a minority of the popular vote, unknown to many of his own party, with no executive experience whatever, mocked at by those who possessed the superficial polish which he lacked, taking office with a bankrupt treasury, a country divided and darkened by approaching war, with incompetence and inexperience everywhere conspicuous, he stood alone upon the threshold of an agonizing crisis, with scarcely one adviser on whose wisdom and devoted loyalty he could perfectly rely. Congress was full of faction: there were those fierce fanatics, the Macbriars and Mucklewraths of Abolitionism, panting for all that was extreme and violent, and looking upon the President as a Gallio whenever he held back from following their frantic lead. There were the War Democrats, patriotic and sincere, but timid, superstitiously shrinking

from anything that savored of extra-constitu-
tional procedure, and reluctant to assent to it
even in the exigencies of a struggle for national existence. There was also a small but
venomous minority made up of those whose
sympathies were really with the South, and
who watched every move of the administration with sleepless vigilance, ready at an instant's notice to pounce upon its errors and
discredit all its counsels. In the Cabinet itself the situation was, if anything, still more
disheartening. The wily, adroit, and immensely able Seward, past-master of political intrigue, could not be expected all at once to
show unqualified devotion to a President who
had defeated him for the nomination that had
been the great ambition of his life. Chase, as
the letters published after his death most plainly show, was thoroughly disloyal, at first de-
spising his chief, and always intriguing against
him. A little later, and Stanton, a life-long
Democrat, a man of violent and arbitrary will,
prone to insubordination and arrogance, introduced into the President's official household
another element of discord. Moreover, thousands of honest but unwisely impatient citizens were fretting at inevitable delay, heart-
sick at the tidings of disaster that came thick

and fast with every bulletin, and ready to be
convinced that the Head of the State was in-
competent or frivolous or shallow.   Add to
this the fact that the passions of all men were
inflamed to the highest pitch, that reason was
stifled, that greed and jobbery and corruption,
starting up in a night at the first breath of
war, throve rankly in every department of the
government, and set their swarms of shame-
less satellites upon the President to beg and
bluster and bedevil.   From such a carnival of
faction and folly the ablest and the purest
might well have shrunk appalled ; the wisest
might have taken up the task and failed without discredit.   But Lincoln, with that clear
vision and that serenity of temper that never
failed him, did not for one moment falter or
complain.   He mastered his Cabinet from the
first, and insured at least its loyalty to the
public service, if not to him ; he compacted
into an efficient legislative entity the inhar-
monious factions of the Congress, yielding a
little here and giving a little there, conciliating
opposition, gently disarming prejudice, always
patient and kindly, but never for a moment
losing sight of the one great end in view, until
at last the fight was won and he stood forth
the absolute master of his party, supreme, un-

challenged, and successful in that victory which was not his victory alone, but first of all his country's. And this was statesmanship.

Yet, if a study of Mr. Cleveland's two administrations should fail to prove his claim to the highest title given to the ruler of a great people, it still yields much that an American may view with quiet satisfaction. That one with little preparation for the task, one who was no student of public affairs, but who was taken almost at random from the mass of ordinary citizens, could still in two great administrative offices display no weakness, but maintain his personal independence; that he could hold his own and make a lasting impression upon the imaginations of his countrymen by his tenacity, his integrity, and his unflinching courage—this fact is one that is distinctly reassuring. Whatever mistakes he may have made, however far he may have fallen short of the highest ideals of statesmanship, his career still shows that the Anglo-Saxon capacity for government everywhere exists in our transplanted race; and so long as this is true, no thoughtful American need ever for one moment despair of the life or of the honor of the Great Republic.

SOME NOTES ON POLITICAL ORATORY

SOME NOTES ON POLITICAL ORATORY

THE recent Presidential nomination by one of the great political parties of a comparatively unknown man because of the impression produced upon the nominating convention by a bit of fervid oratory has, naturally enough, led to an immense amount of discussion as to the present condition and the future possibilities of political eloquence. For quite a number of years it has been taken for granted that the age of oratory has gone by forever; that the time when a brilliant speaker could dominate the minds of a great assemblage will never return; and that the remarkable masters of eloquence whose forensic efforts are as familiar as their names have left behind them no successors whatsoever. Even Professor Sears, in his admirable history of oratory, which is the latest contribution to the serious literature of the subject, speaks of the race of orators as to-day extinct.

The only difference of opinion that has been

manifested has shown itself in an attempt to explain just why great speeches are no longer made. One theory attributes it to a general decline of intellectual ability in our public men, to the tendencies that force into other fields than that of statesmanship the keenest and most brilliant minds of the rising generation, and to a universal drift towards the commonplace and conventional that is depriving modern life, both public and private, of its color and its old-time picturesqueness. The other hypothesis finds the cause in an assumed change that has come over the whole body of our people. We are told that men are more highly trained to-day than in the past; that they are intellectually more self-restrained and less impulsive; that they read more and think more for themselves; and that they are almost universally touched with a certain cynicism and sceptical indifference that render them far less susceptible than formerly to any appeal to their emotions. Hence, it is said, such oratory as survives is in reality little more than business talk, mere logical exposition in which there is no place for the passion and the fire that flamed in the words of a Patrick Henry or a Webster; so that, in our great national forum, Senators and Representatives

alike stand up and read their speeches, or are
contented even with the customary "leave to
print."

One cannot but think that both these explanations are altogether wrong. They utterly
ignore the simpler and more natural solution
to be found in the remarkable change that has
taken place in the nature of the questions that
have now for the past two decades been most
prominent in the sphere of American politics.
For the first time in our national history the
popular thought is centred wholly upon issues
that are absolutely economic and in no sense
sentimental.

In the later colonial period, at which time
the history of American oratory in reality begins, although the question that divided the
colonies from the mother-country was osten-
sibly a question of taxation, the underlying
principle was more profoundly fundamental
and more vital than one of constitutional relations. The thirteen colonies were just beginning to thrill with the half-unconscious stirrings of national life. Men dimly saw within
their grasp the symbols and the splendor of
sovereignty; they felt the strong creative impulse that is always present in the heart of the
Anglo-Saxon; they were rousing themselves

to a recognition of the magnificence of their
future, to the fact that they were no longer
mere colonials, provincials, subjects of a foreign
king, but free men in a free State, with a heritage of unlimited promise and with the power
to claim it and defend it, if necessary, by force
of arms. Therefore, when Patrick Henry and
when Samuel Adams spoke, their words appealed to no sordid sentiment in those who
heard them; but they voiced the aspirations
of an entire people moved to its very heart by
a prophetic consciousness of its own high destiny.

Again, after independence had been achieved
and had finally ceased to be a theme for anything more than occasional oratory, there arose
another issue that involved the strongest possible appeal to sentiment. The question of
slavery in some of its innumerable phases often
appeared to be nothing but a problem of political economy or of constitutional interpretation. For years the leading statesmen of both
parties strove to make it such, to throw it into
the background by compromise and concession,
and to lock the door upon the national skel-
eton. But because it was at base a question
of sentiment, appealing to men's sense of justice and mercy and righteousness, it would not

down; and when it had at last become indis-
solubly linked with still another and even
greater cause—the maintenance of our national
unity and the very life of the Republic—it
stirred the profoundest depths of the nation's
heart.   No more momentous issue was ever
yet evoked in the history of man, for it involved far more than the existence of a single
nation; it concerned the success or failure of
republican government and the fate of free institutions.   No wonder, then, that it inspired
oratory to which the annals of recorded eloquence can find no parallel.   The day when
Webster rose in the Senate of the United
States to deliver, amid a silence like that of
death, his marvellous reply to Hayne, may well
be thought the most memorable and momentous in the whole history of the American Republic.   And the speech of Webster was in
every word and every line fully up to the sublime level of the issues it discussed.   It is no
exaggeration to say that it overtops any other
effort of human eloquence that the world has
known.*   Its only rival is the oration of Demosthenes on the Crown; and this, I think,

* Lest this be thought extravagant, it may be interesting
to note that the Lord Chief Justice of England, Baron Russell
of Killowen, himself a finished orator, declared to an Ameri-

holding strictly to the attitude of dispassionate criticism, must take the second place. In patriotic fervor, in sincerity, in absolute mastery of the resources of rhetoric, and in intellectual power, the two great orators were equal; but from the stand-point of historical importance, and, above all, in the vastness of the ultimate consequences, the Greek must yield to the American. For in the case of Demosthenes the issue was immediately personal; in the case of Webster the issue was distinctly national. Demosthenes was defending and extenuating a political failure; Webster was pointing the way to a national triumph. The greatness upon which Demosthenes so fondly dwelt was retrospective; the greatness that Webster limned before his breathless hearers lay in the living present and the future. One statesman appealed to a proud and melancholy memory; the other to a splendid aspiration. One was pronouncing a stately funeral oration; the other was sounding a great trumpet-call to victory. And in the actual results achieved there can be no comparison. Athenian liberty was already dead, and no words, however elo-

can friend some little time ago that in his opinion Webster was, on the whole, the greatest master of eloquence of whom the world has any record.

quent, could bring it back to life. But American nationality was just feeling its first vigorous, vital impulse. The words of Demosthenes
could, at the best, awaken in the mind of an
Athenian nothing more than a sombre stirring
of humiliation and regret for a past forever
gone; the words of Webster, committed to
memory and declaimed by generations of
American children, sank down into the hearts
of his countrymen until his closing sentence
became the very watchword of the Republic,
and until the great principle for which he spoke
had been learned so thoroughly that when the
years of storm and stress arrived a million men
stood ready to pour out their blood like water,
and a million mothers sent forth their sons with
gladness to die in its defence. And the oration
itself—what a wonderful thing it is! Its dignified and graceful exordium, its stately sentences moving on with an ever-growing impetus
and throbbing with a joyous consciousness of
irresistible power, its passion and pathos, its
majestic rhythm and cadenced harmonies rising and sinking like a grand organ-roll or the
thunder of the sea, and finally the magnificent
sunburst of gorgeous imagery with which it
ends! Even now, after more than sixty years
have passed, and after the issues that inspired

18

it have been laid at rest forever, no American
who deserves the name can read over those tremendous sentences without feeling his pulses
quicken and his heart thrill with an exultant
emotion so keen as to be almost pain.

As for Cicero, it would be absurd to com-
pare him as an orator with either of the others.
The fatal insincerity of character that taints
his utterances makes some of his most elaborate orations, in spite of their rhetorical perfection, seem cheap and thin when set beside
the massive eloquence of Demosthenes and
Webster; his impassioned declamation too
often suggests the actor's rant; his invective
and his pathos at times come perilously near
to the neurotic caterwauling of an hysterical
woman.

Oratory naturally found a powerful stimulus
in the Civil War and in the questions immediately arising from it; and for many years
thereafter it was always possible for the political speaker to stir his hearers by calling up
once more the memories and the passions of
that gigantic conflict. But as a new generation came upon the scene and as other issues
gradually forced their way to the front, eloquence was tamed. When the phrase, "waving
the bloody shirt," was once coined, it marked

the end of the oratory that fed upon martial
themes. Since 1880 the minds of the people
have been fixed with more and more persist-
ence upon the economic and financial policy
of the country; and in this sphere there is
little food for forensic eloquence. The sched-
ules of a tariff are not inspiring to a popular
orator; barbed wire and jute and cotton ties,
and the relative merits of ad valorem and
specific duties, cannot possibly be worked up
into rhetorical material even by the most ingenious pleader. Nor is the financial question
much more promising. There are persons, indeed, who have dwelt with harrowing detail
upon the wrongs and sufferings of silver, and
who have depicted in tones of horror the cowardice and the malevolence of gold ; but the
oratorical effect has not been striking. It is
very difficult to draw tears from a hard-headed
American crowd over the injuries and sorrows
of a metal; nor will many persons rage together because of the depravity of something
that can be represented by a chemical symbol.
It is only when a more direct and personal
turn can be given to the theme that an orator
has any chance of real success. This is pretty
well illustrated in Mr. Bryan's now memorable speech at Chicago in July, 1896. Had he

dwelt, as did the opposing speakers, upon the purely economic side of the question, he would have left the convention as cold as they did. He therefore deliberately chose to make the issue a sectional one : to pit the West against the East ; to describe in impassioned language the honest farmer in his peaceful home ground down by malevolent oppressors, at whom the orator flung a fierce defiance. In other words, he turned a question of finance into a question of pure sentiment. As to the justice or the wisdom or the patriotism of this device, we are not here concerned ; but from the orator-ical point of view it was very shrewd, and it showed that Mr. Bryan possessed the orator-ical instinct in a very high degree.   Its success was, indeed, its justification ; for as the sole aim of the orator is to master his audience and play upon their feelings until he can bend them to his will, oratory is the one thing of which the only criterion is success. The same remark applies to the substance of this speech, which has been criticised as tawdry, stilted, and even blasphemous; but which (ethical considerations apart) was, in fact, rhetorically perfect as being exactly suited to the state of mind of those who heard it and were mastered by it.

It is reasonable to suppose, therefore, that the present lack of oratory of a startling and dramatic kind is due neither to any decline in oratorical ability on the part of our public speakers, nor to any loss of impressibility on the part of the American people — certainly not to the latter, for there is ample evidence that as a nation we are becoming more rather than less emotional, more nervous, more excitable.   But when the themes of oratory are not those that feed popular passion, the born orator pitches his utterances in a low key and subdues his whole discourse to the natural level of his subject.   In fact, it is in this very thing that his real genius is best seen ; for precisely in proportion to his greatness will an unerring instinct teach him to shun any attempt to elevate by purely rhetorical devices a theme that is in itself essentially commonplace.   Hence it is that the ablest of our speakers to-day are just the ones who never force the note, but wisely prefer to leave upon their hearers the impression embodied in the fine Horatian description

> urbani parcentis viribus atque
> Extenuantis eas consulto ;

and those who neglect this precept often come

perilously near the line where declamation passes into rant.

It is in this respect that the public speakers of the South are so curiously defective. As a class, they seem to think that any subject whatsoever can be made impressive provided it be plastered thick with a multiplicity of gaudy adjectives, bedizened with innumerable metaphors, and daubed all over with the raddle of rhetorical rouge. These men sow with the sack and not with the hand, and believe that they have hit upon an infallible formula for producing "eloquence" to order. I have in mind the Chief Executive of one of the oldest and stateliest of the Southern States, whose speeches are the *reductio ad absurdum* of this barbaric style. Whether he is delivering an inaugural address, or whether he is speaking over the pumpkins at a county fair, his verbal pyrotechnics are such that if I were to set down one of his passages in cold type most readers would suspect that I had invented it in a spirit of the wildest and most farcical burlesque. I do not know just how such oratory is generally regarded in the South. If it is taken seriously and viewed with admiration, the fact is a lamentable indication of the condition of public taste and of the

lack of any wide-spread æsthetic cultivation;
for were such a speaker to dress in a manner to harmonize with his oratorical style,
he would appear before his audiences array-
ed in a nose-ring and an inch of vermilion
paint.

It must be confessed, however, that the
South has no monopoly of this half-savage
sort of pow-wow. All the national conventions held in 1896 provided choice specimens
of it in nominating speeches that fairly knocked the bottom out of the vocabulary of eulogy,
when some backwoods lawyer, unknown even
to many of the delegates from his own State,
would be described as " the peerless jurist, the
profound scholar, the magnificent and electri-
fying orator, the world's greatest statesman
and thinker!" At such utterances as these,
pronounced before deliberative bodies that are
supposed to shape the nation's policy and select its rulers, the self-respecting American can
only blush for the credit of the Republic.

It is, indeed, in the subtle instinct that tells
just how the discourse is to be attuned to the
mood of the moment that the true orator is
ultimately to be distinguished from the mere
rhetorician. Nice judgment, perfect tact, and
an innate sense of what is possible to be ac-

complished in a given situation have often
done far more for a reputation than the actual
arts of eloquence.   A contemporaneous illustration may be found in Mr. Bryan's address
at the Madison Square Garden, in this city, in
reply to the Committee of Notification, which
is an excellent case in point.   His passionate
harangue at Chicago and its remarkable effect
on his immediate hearers had led every one to
expect an equally fiery oration in New York;
yet when he appeared before the great assem-
bly that had gathered to receive him, he simply read a written essay with no attempt at
eloquence whatever.   His political opponents
at once raised a howl of derision, and even
many of his own supporters were for the moment much chagrined.   Yet this was in reality one of the cleverest things that he had
ever done ; and the reason for this opinion is
perfectly obvious.   In the interval between
his Chicago speech and the time set for his
New York address, public expectation had
been worked up to so extravagant a pitch that
had he been Demosthenes and Cicero rolled
into one he could not possibly have satisfied
it.   He therefore very wisely declined to attempt what, from the conditions, was fore-
doomed to failure — declined, in fact, to com-

pete against himself. To be sure, by reading
an essay instead of delivering an oration, he
disappointed his auditors, and he was gibed
by the opposition press; but he did not for-
feit his reputation as an orator, and this seem-
ing fiasco made an admirable background for
any brilliant and effective speeches that he
might subsequently deliver.

Political orations in general may be classified under three heads. First come those
great efforts that are overwhelming in their
effect at the time of their delivery, and that
stand the test of time so well as even now to
be read with genuine pleasure and admiration.
Next come the speeches that produce no great
effect upon their immediate hearers, but that
subsequently, by reason of their literary merit,
take high rank among the classics of the language in which they are composed. Finally,
there are the orations that serve their purpose
at the time, or that win a temporary renown
by reason of the occasion on which they were
delivered, or because of the personal charm
and impressiveness of the orator, but which are
afterwards of little interest except as affording
material for the historian. To the first class
belong the greatest speeches of Demosthenes,
of Webster, of Cicero, and perhaps of Lincoln.

Of the second class a type may be found in the parliamentary orations of Burke, who always emptied the House of Commons when he spoke, but whose loftiness of thought and splendor of diction have won for him a lasting place in the annals of political eloquence. To the third class belong the great mass of political orations in all ages and all countries. Such are the speeches of Henry Clay, in reading which one marvels at the effect which we know to have been produced by them, of Hayne and Benton and Everett and Legaré, of J. P. Hale and Sumner and Stevens, and, in fact, of pretty nearly all the American orators of the past fifty years.

In this country the public estimate of living orators is seldom accurate, because it is so warped and biassed by partisan prejudice. It is, moreover, largely influenced by the newspapers, which usually carry their criticism of the substance into condemnation of the form. Seldom, indeed, does a Democratic journal see anything to admire in the oratory of a Republican statesman; and in estimating the merit of a Democratic speaker, the Republican critics almost invariably (to use the time-honored expression) "dismiss it with a smile." Consequently, it is not until death has blunted the

sharpness of political acrimony that anything
like a truthful estimate is ever formed, and
even then it may be many years before the
exaggerations of both partisan panegyric and
partisan depreciation have fully passed away.

It is probable, for instance, that among all
the orators of the past two decades public
opinion at the present time would ascribe a
marked supremacy to Mr. Blaine. Yet it is
certain that it was not primarily as an orator
that Mr. Blaine secured and kept his remarkable influence over the host of those who followed so loyally his personal and political
fortunes. Mr. Blaine had, to be sure, the orator's temperament. He was mentally alert,
quick to seize upon an effective point, impet-
uous, and in his early career full of fire. He
had an unusual command of the resources of
language, and unfailing tact and taste. Yet
the fact remains that it was not through oratory that he won the commanding position
which he held in his party's counsels, nor did
he rely upon it to any great extent in carry-
ing out his political ambitions. The reason is
not far to seek. It is found in the fact that
very early in his career he set before himself
the presidency as the goal of his ambition,
and with this always in mind he purposely

modified and restrained his natural bent in
many ways. Now Mr. Blaine was by nature
an exceedingly impulsive man, one whose temperament led him to form decisions with light-
ninglike rapidity, and to act upon them with
unchecked and unreflecting impetuosity. In
this quality of mind lay at once his strength
and his weakness, and to it his greatest successes and his greatest mistakes are alike directly traceable. Had he been content to
limit his ambition to anything short of the
highest office in the nation's gift, he would undoubtedly have let his oratorical talent have
full play, and would have deserved the reputation for eloquence that is now, I think,
unreasonably given him. It was, to be sure,
by a spirited and brilliant speech that he won
his first great national distinction, while still
a member of the House of Representatives.
The occasion was a debate upon the question
of granting a complete political amnesty to
Jefferson Davis, in spite of the fact that Mr.
Davis himself had never asked for it. Mr.
Blaine opposed the measure, and Mr. Hill, of
Georgia, one of the very ablest of the Southern
leaders, stood forth as its champion and de-
fender. In the spirited debate that followed,
Mr. Blaine gave full play to his impetuosity.

With no preparation and no premeditation, he
flung himself into the forensic combat, and in
a burst of vivid oratory fanned again the fires
of sectional feeling which had begun to smoul-
der, but which at his words once more flamed
up as fiercely as in the days of the Civil War.
The whole North thrilled at his passionate appeal, and in an hour his name was in all men's
mouths.   It was the victory of a partisan, but
it was magnificent nevertheless; and the memory of it led Colonel Ingersoll a few years
later, in an almost equally celebrated speech,
to style him "the Plumed Knight," a title that
presently became hackneyed in the vocabulary
of the stump. Yet never again did Mr. Blaine
fully give way to an oratorical impulse such
as this.   Experience and keen self-analysis
taught him the danger that lay in his own impetuosity, and from the moment when he first
formed a definite ambition to be President he
set a bridle on his tongue. His speeches thereafter were able, ingenious, and adequate, but,
to the present writer at least, there seemed always to run through them a certain tone of
calculation, of conscious design half verging
upon craft, that robbed them of their spontaneity and greatly marred their psychological
effect. The speaker seemed always to be keep-

ing something back, to withhold a part of his
confidence, to be playing with his audience as
a cat plays with a mouse, and to be very far
indeed from the perfect self-abandonment that
marks the inspired orator.

Mr. Blaine's great influence as a party leader
sprang, in fact, from a deeper source than verbal eloquence.   Men early began to speak of
his "magnetism," and the word speedily entered into the slang of our politics.   It was, in
consequence, so harped upon and burlesqued as
to become a mere vulgarism of party speech ;
yet, for want of a better word, it must still be
used to express the secret of his power.   Its
real meaning, however, is not so often understood.   The popular conception of a "mag-
netic" leader is of one who wins adherents by
a jovial bearing, by a sort of hail-fellow-well-
met jollity, of which few statesmen were ever
more guiltless than Mr. Blaine—a model of
personal dignity in all his relations with his
friends and followers.   By his "magnetism"
we should rather understand a certain power
that he exercised, through those immediately
in contact with him, upon great masses of men
who had never seen him, so that they, too,
became irresistibly convinced of his incompa-
rable fitness for command.   The manifestation

of this power is a curious psychological study,
and may be illustrated in a statement made to
the present writer by an official of the State
Department at the time when Mr. Blaine was
Secretary.   This gentleman, who was, by the
way, politically opposed to Mr. Blaine, said
that every morning the various officials of the
department would be at work upon their usual
tasks, going through them in the leisurely way
that is traditional in this particular division of
the public service, chatting amicably together,
yawning, pausing to scan the morning paper,
and in general accomplishing a minimum of
work in a maximum of time.   Suddenly, for
no reason that any one could explain, a sort
of impulse comparable to an electric shock
would run through the assemblage.   Conversation would cease, newspapers would be laid
aside, pens would fly over the paper, the whole
work of the department would all at once pro-
ceed with intense celerity.   No one had been
heard to enter the next room, not a word of
warning had been spoken, yet every one in
the place knew by an inexplicable instinct that
Mr. Blaine was in his office.

This strange power is probably a natural attribute of the born leader of men.   It was possessed in a large degree by General Grant, a

man who, in temperament, training, and mental
processes, was the very antithesis of Mr. Blaine.
Old army officers often tell of their experiences in 1863, when the newly promoted soldier was put in command of the troops who
were ultimately to operate against Vicksburg.
Previous attempts against the Confederate
stronghold had failed disastrously, and sol-
diers and officers alike were thoroughly dis-
heartened.   There was a general inefficiency
in the staff, and a general lack of system,
order, and discipline throughout the army.
Plans were made and unmade ; regiments were
marched aimlessly backwards and forwards;
supplies went to the wrong place ; everything,
in fact, was at sixes and sevens.   This was the
state of things when it was announced that
General Grant had been put in command.   Old
officers shrugged their shoulders.   Here was
more experimenting.   A new general meant
to them only a new element of confusion.   On
a certain day Grant assumed command, but not
immediately at general headquarters.   No one
had yet seen him when, before forty-eight hours
had elapsed, in some indefinable way a curious
change came over the whole army.   An invisi-
ble power made itself felt in every department.
Definite purpose began to appear in every

move. Supplies appeared when they were
wanted. The troops were swung into intelligible combinations. Everywhere precision,
order, discipline reigned where before there
had been only confusion, chaos, insubordination. And when things were seen to be actually *done*, the most inveterate grumbler on the
staff stood up in the midst of his fellow-officers
and, slapping his leg, roared out with a sort of
Homeric joy, " At last! at last! By heavens,
at last they have given us a MAN!"

Therefore, it is by no means correct to lay
too much stress on Mr. Blaine's oratory as the
chief factor in his political supremacy. It was
rather his resourcefulness, his tact, his constructive power, his " magnetism," that secured to him his unquestioned leadership.
Not but what his speeches were admirable
efforts, from the purely political addresses
that he made in the campaign of 1876 and
1880 to the elaborate and dignified oration
pronounced by him before the President, the
Houses of Congress, and the Diplomatic Corps
on the death of President Garfield. The brief
addresses, too, that he made in his own canvass for the Presidency in 1884 were admirable in their point and tact and persuasiveness;
though it was this campaign that extinguish-

19

ed his oratory altogether. The extraordinary labor that he took upon himself, the excitement and fatigue, and more than all else perhaps, his exasperating defeat by a few hundred votes in a single State, quenched the fire of his ambition, and left him a disappointed and almost broken man. He spoke again in the campaign of 1888, but while his intellect was as active as before, his physical strength had been sapped, so that his every sentence seemed to involve an obvious and painful effort. The orator, like the actor, needs, above all else, to overflow with an abundant and vigorous vitality, because, like the actor, the impression that he makes is in no small degree a physical impression. Yet it was not merely in bodily force that Mr. Blaine's great defeat impaired his power. There was a marked deterioration in manner and in temper perceptible during his last few years that can, perhaps, be most clearly seen in some of his state papers, and notably in his diplomatic controversy with Lord Salisbury concerning the American claim to jurisdiction in Behring Sea. The traditions of diplomacy require the tone of all formal communications to be ceremonious and courtly to the last degree. The question at issue may be of the most burning kind, the contro-

versy may be even of the sort that inevitably
ends in war, yet nevertheless the diplomatic
duellists must everywhere observe the most
punctilious etiquette, and never in word or
phrase overstep the limits of a stately self-
restraint.   These traditions Lord Salisbury,
on his side, observed to the full.   His immensely able argument was couched throughout in terms of the finest courtesy, suggesting
in every line the urbanity and the graceful
deference that mark the intercourse of high-
bred gentlemen.   But Mr. Blaine's despatches,
whatever be their plausibility and force, are
very painful reading.   There is observable in
them here and there a certain swagger, a half-
rowdy tone of lurking insolence, an offensive
assumption that his opponent's argument is
one of conscious duplicity and falsehood.   It
is not likely that our diplomatic records contain another correspondence such as this.
Some may advance against this view and in
defence of Mr. Blaine the once famous Hülse-
mann Letter, written to the Austrian Minister
by Daniel Webster when Secretary of State,
and resenting the attempted protest of Austria
against our Government's very obvious sympathies with the Hungarian insurgents.   But
this letter, in which many persons, in total dis-

regard of chronology, have seen the original suggestion of the " Pogram Defiance " in *Martin Chuzzlewit*, while it was, to be sure, rather startlingly unconventional, and, on the whole, rather bumptious in its manner, contained not a word that could give the slightest personal offence to its recipient.

There is something of the irony of fate in the circumstance that, after years of studied discretion in word and act, the careless speech of a stranger should have been so largely instrumental in marring the one great ambition of Mr. Blaine's career.   There is something almost tragic, too, in the thought of all that long-continued effort, all that eager hope, all that fertility of resource, and all those brilliant gifts just failing of supreme success.   The present writer saw Mr. Blaine four days before the election that was to set the seal of failure on his remarkable career.   It was at the very end of the campaign, and he was on his way to some small city in Connecticut to make one last address.   He sat by the open window of the railway-carriage waiting for the train to start.   His head was bent forward, and the sunken eyes, the face blanched to an ashen pallor, and the pinched and jaded features all told the tale of mental weariness and physical

exhaustion. A knot of a dozen or twenty
men, who had gathered on the platform, stared
curiously at him ; and now and then, as one or
another of them approached and offered to
shake hands, Mr. Blaine would thrust three
fingers through the window and force a wan,
mechanical smile. It reminded one of nothing
half so much as of some hunted animal driven
to its hole and turning feebly to eye its unfeel-
ing persecutors. Could the very bitterest of
his enemies have beheld him then, and could
they have foreseen the impending wreck of his
life's one great ambition, they must have felt
some stirrings of pity, and, it may be, even of
remorse ; for the sight was infinitely pathetic,
and one to haunt the memory for many days.

The extent to which false estimates of living orators gain popular acceptance through
newspaper influence can be very well illustrated in the case of Mr. Roscoe Conkling.   Mr.
Conkling was a fair speaker, no better and no
worse than scores of others who in his day
and generation were heard upon the floor of
Congress.   His best efforts were those of the
earlier part of his senatorial career, during the
Reconstruction Period ; but if any one will take
the trouble to consult the files of the *Congressional Record*, he will find that, while Mr. Conk-

ling often spoke with a good deal of ability, and sometimes with considerable force and point, there is nothing in his speeches to mark him out as oratorically pre-eminent among the other political leaders of that day, and that not a few of his contemporaries easily surpassed him. He was, for instance, markedly inferior to the late Matthew H. Carpenter, of Wisconsin, a very brilliant and effective debater, though by the present generation wellnigh forgotten. Nevertheless, from the beginning of President Grant's first administration, in 1869, down to the time of his own death, in 1888, Mr. Conkling was singled out by the newspaper press for the most extravagant laudation as being one of the most impressive, stirring, and convincing orators of the day. Even now it is a sort of tradition in newspaper offices, and therefore in the minds of a large number of intelligent Americans, that Mr. Conkling's name is always to be mentioned in enumerating our great masters of political eloquence. Mr. Conkling's oratorical reputation, in fact, is mainly the artificial creation of a prolonged and elaborate newspaper " boom."

Now, the original inventors of this myth were undoubtedly sincere believers in it; and those who afterwards accepted it did so largely as a matter of faith in an established tradition. The explanation of the thing is a twofold explanation. The first reason is found in Mr. Conkling's personality ; the second in the influence that he was able to exert through certain fortunate political connections. Mr. Conkling, as every one knows, was a man of rather striking presence, powerful in build, and one who always sought to make the most of his own physical advantages. He was, indeed, excessively vain, dressing in a way to attract attention, continually posing for the admiration of the galleries, and doing everything with an air that was meant to be impressive and that did impress a good many inexperienced persons who were unable accurately to distinguish between swaggering arrogance and the dignity that is the accompaniment of real power. Whenever he made a formal speech, the way for it was prepared as carefully as when a dramatist works up a situation to afford an effective entrance for the leading actor. Mr. Conkling's strut, his portentous frown, his dramatic gestures, and even the arrangement of his famous curl were all studied out by him as minutely as his Roman prototype, Hortensius, is said to have studied out the arrangement of the folds in his forensic toga. Mr. Blaine, in fact, in the very celebrated speech that made Conkling his implacable enemy for life, found in this display of personal vanity the feather that winged his sharpest shaft. This speech, whose studied antitheses prove it to have been no impromptu sally, but a carefully prepared attack, must be regarded as wholly unparliamentary, and, in view of the place in which it was delivered, as lacking in the very first elements of good taste; while throughout its whole comparison of Mr. Conkling with Henry Winter Davis it extravagantly overrated Davis and was in reality too severe upon Conkling, yet there was so large an element of truth in its characterization as to make it rankle in the latter's memory down to the very day of his death. The comparison of Mr. Conkling to a turkey-cock was at once caught up by all the political cartoonists, and thereafter the strut and the pompous pose appeared and reappeared in a pictorial form as ludicrous as it was felicitous. Mr. Conkling's theatric self-assertion, however, though repellent to most persons of refined taste, did nevertheless impose upon a great many people, inasmuch as the world at large generally takes a man at his own valuation; and the newspaper correspondents in particular were deeply im-

pressed by his airs and graces. They spoke
and wrote of him habitually as "Lord Roscoe,"
and regarded his swagger as superb. The
power, too, which at this time he undoubtedly
wielded may be taken as affording some excuse for their delusion. President Grant, who
was rather famous for his misjudgment of men
in civil life, gave his personal and political
friendship to Mr. Conkling, and by allowing
him to dictate the federal appointments in the
State of New York, enabled him to play for
several years the congenial *rôle* of political dictator. Thus with those who saw his "Olym-
pian" bearing apparently quite justified by his
possession of acquired power, there grew up
an unquestioning belief in his greatness, and
the tradition survived the wreck of his political fortunes.

It was said of Mr. Conkling that while in
Washington he had made himself proficient in
boxing, and that he took the greatest delight
in getting some inexperienced friend, who had
not heard of his accomplishment, to put on the
gloves for an amicable bout with him. Then
would he buffet the unfortunate man most un-
mercifully, and feel an exquisite joy in his own
vast superiority as he knocked his victim about
the room. This was a very characteristic trait,

because it was so typical of a bully's nature. That he was, in fact, a bully was made perfectly clear in many of the most important crises of his public life—a bully in his attempts to browbeat his way to the attainment of his ends, and a bully in his conduct when he encountered a firm and manly opposition.

The way in which he took Mr. Blaine's oratorical attack upon him is an excellent illustration, for it is the very first virtue of a politician to accept with good-nature the punishment that he may receive in the course of his public career, and not to bear malice for any length of time; whereas Mr. Conkling never forgave this verbal chastisement which he had neither the courage nor the ability to answer at the time, but which he stored up vindictively in his memory to make of it an excuse for many exhibitions of petty spite throughout the rest of his career.

Another lamentable revelation of his real nature was that which he made before the Rochester Convention in 1877, when, on certain questions of party policy, he came into conflict with Mr. George William Curtis, the gentlest, most dignified, and most courteous of men, and made a personal attack upon him which went completely over the line that sepa-

rates oratorical invective from ordinary black-
guardism. Mr. Conkling's biographer, in chron-
icling this unpleasant incident, quotes a eulogy
upon the speech from the columns of a newspaper which regards it as one of the greatest
in the whole annals of oratory, and compares
Mr. Conkling with Pitt, Burke, and Sheridan;
but the biographer himself, while professing to
reproduce the speech in full, expunges, out of
shame, some of its phrases, and supplies their
place with asterisks.

Again, every one remembers his arrogant
attempt, in the early days of the Garfield administration, to impose his will upon the President and to stretch the senatorial prerogative
until it should overshadow and in part destroy
the independence of the Executive. Had it
been only the amiable Garfield who confronted
him in this attempt, he might have succeeded;
but here again, behind the President, stood his
old antagonist, Mr. Blaine, then Secretary of
State—cool, watchful, a master of fence, and
wielding a weapon whose perfect temper made
Conkling, with his clumsy bludgeon, appear the
veriest tyro. Unable to carry his point, the
Senator, like a sulky school-boy, resigned his
seat, in the hope of a "vindication" at the
hands of the New York Legislature, and there-

by played into the hands of his opponent, who skilfully blocked the "vindication," and in the end brought about Mr. Conkling's political downfall.

Yet, in spite of all these revelations of himself, the tradition of his greatness still survived, until the myth obtained a final lodgment in the imagination of his countrymen, and the tradition itself has now become a fixed belief in the minds of a great majority of the American people.

If Mr. Conkling affords a good instance of an orator whose reputation has been unduly exalted in the popular mind, Senator Hill, of New York, may be taken as one who, on the whole, has had scant justice done him. This, also, is quite easily accounted for. A good deal of prejudice has sprung up in estimating his ability as a public speaker, from the circumstance, now pretty generally admitted to be true, that he has at times delivered addresses that were not wholly original with himself—to put it plainly, that he has sometimes had his speeches written for him. Accepting this assertion as a fact, some explanation is necessary to show that in reality it should not seriously affect one's judgment of such speeches as are beyond any question all his own.

In the first place, if the truth were known, it would probably be found that Mr. Hill is by no means singular in availing himself of another's aid in getting up some of his formal speeches. And though in our own country such a thing is generally held to be rather discreditable to an orator, in other countries it is accepted as a very ordinary incident. Few European monarchs, for example, ever make a speech of their own composition, but impressively pronounce the words that are carefully prepared for them by their Ministers of State; nor is this necessarily due to any inability on their part to give a fit expression to their own ideas, but because, having often to speak in places and on subjects of which they have themselves no minutely accurate knowledge, they make use of the special experience of other men, lest by some careless phrase or indiscreet allusion they should give unintentional offence. The only exception that one easily recalls is the German Kaiser, whose utterances are absolutely his own, and are, from an oratorical point of view, often extremely picturesque and stirring. Yet this very exception affords a strong justification of the rule adopted by his brother sovereigns; for all Europe is uneasy whenever it is known that he is

expected to make a speech, and every one can
recall a dozen instances when the over-frank
expressions of the hare-brained War Lord have
not only given grievous offence to other gov-
ernments, but have excited the bitterest resentment among large sections of his own subjects.

The rule holds good, also, of many personages whose position is less political than ornamental. The Prince of Wales, for instance, a
hundred times a year is expected to preside
at functions where a speech from him is necessary—now at the meeting of a charitable society, now at the opening of a hospital, now at
a dinner of artists or literary men or scientists,
and now at some ceremonial more closely connected with the immediate interests of the
State. It would be impossible for him to speak
with pertinence and accuracy upon so many
subjects requiring special knowledge and often
special tact; and, as a matter of fact, upon
every one of these occasions his innocuous
little speech is carefully prepared for him beforehand by some discreet person who understands the situation and is able to infuse into
the address the necessary amount of technical
allusion and local appropriateness. Every one
in England fully understands this, though the

newspapers cherish a decorous fiction by occasional bursts of perfunctory enthusiasm over the Prince's gifts as a versatile and tactful speaker. In private, however, no one thinks it worth while to adopt this superstition, and the present writer knows of one individual who was once invited to prepare an address for the Prince to deliver before a gathering of archæologists, and who, since then, pretty nearly always manages to bring a conversation around to the point where he can inform the company of the vast honor that was done him in asking him to play the part of oratorical jackal to his Royal Highness. Nor is this vicarious eloquence despised by foreign statesmen generally. When the subject on which they have to speak is one in which they are personally interested or with which they are already especially familiar, they trust to their own resources and their own inspiration ; but in other cases the departmental clerk or the convenient, and often very able, private secretary gets up the facts and provides the backbone of the speech, and frequently also much of its actual flesh and blood, in the way of argument and phrase and rhetorical embellishment. It is likely, too, that, as said above, our own statesmen are not in reality so very

different from their foreign brethren. One
of the oldest and most respected members
of Congress once showed me the manuscript
of an address that he was going to deliver
on the subject of the tariff, and casually remarked:

"My son-in-law did that, and a very good
speech it is, too."

The writer ventured to ask, knowing him
very well, whether all his political speeches
were from the same source.

"Oh no," he answered. "Only, you see, I
don't care a straw myself about the tariff question, and he is full of it ; so I just asked him
to get up the speech."

Consequently, it must not be viewed as a
serious charge against Mr. Hill if he has followed the many distinguished precedents that
are at hand.   There is in his case a broad distinction to be drawn between the various orations that he has from time to time delivered ;
and this line of demarcation is to be fixed by
remembering a perfectly obvious truth in connection with his political career.   Mr. Hill's
early training and his long possession of party
leadership in the State of New York produced
a very natural effect in making the politics of
that State more personally interesting to him

than those which are connected with national affairs. He is in this respect the natural successor of Mr. Tilden, knowing thoroughly every district of the State, every local politician of importance, the history of every issue and of every movement for a quarter of a century; and he can gauge to a dot the motives and the measures of enemy and friend alike. This sort of thing has by many been described in a contemptuous but rather telling phrase as " peanut politics"; yet those who use the term forget that New York State, with its fifty thousand square miles of area, its six millions of inhabitants, its enormous wealth, and its vast commercial interests, is a political entity of far greater importance than many of the minor European kingdoms; and that what they sneer at in Mr. Hill they would commend as statesmanship in a Dutch or Danish or Norwegian politician. It is, in fact, only by comparison with the immensity of our whole great national domain that the local interests of New York seem relatively unimportant.

However this may be, it is certain that Mr. Hill, when first elected to the Senate, went very reluctantly to Washington, and only as a *pis aller;* that for a long time he felt politically homesick in his new and untried sur-

20

roundings; and that, as was entirely natural, he could not all at once get fully into touch with the men and the measures that he had hitherto, like the rest of us, looked at only from a distance. Consequently, when it became necessary for Senator Hill to speak upon questions that were still to him comparatively unfamiliar, he felt a very natural mistrust of his own ability to avoid the pitfalls that were certain to be dug for him; and if he then availed himself of another's aid we need not blame him overmuch. That which does, however, call for censure is the wretched choice he must have made of a collaborator, for the first set speech pronounced by him before the Senate is one of the most ghastly things that the records of Congressional oratory can show. In it Mr. Hill was so ill-advised as to attempt a humorous *rôle*, and to string together a lot of wretched puns upon the names of the leading New York newspapers—the *Sun*, the *World*, the *Times*, the *Tribune*, and so forth — the effect of which was painful and pathetic to a degree. Even the opposition journals passed it over lightly, so melancholy was the spectacle that the Senator afforded; and they gave him the benefit of the charity which men accord to those who have lately died.

Mr. Hill never again made himself responsible for anything so unfortunate as this ; yet one may, in general, set aside, when considering his oratorical ability, those speeches that belong to the period of his first entrance upon the field of national politics. In them he had to do with themes that had not yet begun to interest him, and in discussing them he showed the intellectual *gaucherie* of one who is ill at ease amid unusual surroundings.

It is not likely that there are many who really lay much stress upon Mr. Hill's ability as an orator, no matter what his subject ; and if oratory be so defined as to include only the impassioned and emotional forms of public speaking, then there is little or nothing to be said in his behalf. But no such restricted definition is reasonable ; and with a broader standard of judgment it is likely that Mr. Hill deserves some serious consideration as an orator. Whenever he has had to advocate a policy which concerned the things that were nearest to his own heart, or to defend a course of action taken by him in relation to the affairs of his own State, he has shown no small power of exposition and argument and persuasion. When, as Governor, he from time to time addressed great audiences on State affairs, he often rose to a high level. The theme was a congenial one; he knew it thoroughly; and his audiences were gathered, not to be amazed or thrilled or startled, but to be convinced. Under such conditions Mr. Hill's efforts were models of earnest, lucid, and straightforward speech, and their effect in gaining him a popular support was undeniable. A life-long Republican, who is also a gentleman of great cultivation and critical ability, once met the present writer soon after attending a meeting at which Governor Hill had spoken, and, in answer to a question, said:

" He seems to me to speak with very great ability and force, and after hearing him I am convinced that he is thoroughly sincere."

Now, as political sincerity is the very last virtue with which Mr. Hill's enemies would be willing to credit him, it must be admitted that to produce an impression such as this upon a prejudiced opponent is evidence of genuine oratorical power. It was, however, a great tactical mistake when, at the Chicago Convention of 1896, Mr. Hill was put forward by the gold men as their chief orator. Wholly unimpassioned at all times, excitement on the part of those about him seems always to make him colder and more unbend-

ing still, and on this occasion his manner was
one of absolute frigidity. The address he made
was wholly argumentative, a pure appeal to
reason, and one which, if pronounced before
a deliberative body, would have had considerable weight. But in these days a national convention is no longer a deliberative body. With
the galleries packed by a yelling mob, and the
floor filled by a surging mass of delegates frantic with excitement, mere argument and reason
make no impression ; and only the orator who
can appeal to sentiment and passion can ob-
tain the mastery, and rule by the power of
words that burn and blaze their way to the
mind through the path of the emotions.

It is doubtful whether even the warmest
friends of ex-President Cleveland regard him as
an orator; and it may therefore seem a waste
of time to speak of him in dealing with a subject such as this. Nothing, indeed, could be
more remote from eloquence than his infrequent political addresses. Couched in poly-
syllabic words that clumsily clog themselves
into sentences of more than Johnsonian pon-
derosity, Mr. Cleveland's ideas when given in
a public speech are nearly always found to
be distinctly platitudinous. That the citizen
should always cherish virtue, that unbridled

selfishness and greed are serious dangers to
the body politic, that intelligence and public
spirit are especially desirous in a Republic—
such are the by no means startling and original thoughts that appear and reappear in Mr.
Cleveland's deliverances. The only question
that arises in one's mind is whether this enumeration of the baldest truisms must be accepted as the best thing that the ex-President
can do in the way of oratory, or whether this
style has been deliberately selected by him as
being ultimately the wisest means of accomplishing a distinct and definite object. It has
been very shrewdly pointed out (I think by
Mr. E. L. Godkin) that for a statesman who is
seeking public confidence rather than popular
admiration, this rather tame and unoriginal
vein is exceedingly judicious; and I am inclined to believe that there is much to be said
in favor of such an hypothesis. There is nothing, in fact, that the average citizen so much
distrusts as mere brilliancy in a public man.
He is not brilliant himself, and he has a vague
suspicion that one who is so extremely clever
may be altogether too clever to be trusted.
He will admire him immensely, but he will be
always just the least bit afraid of him. On
the other hand, a statesman who is prosaic, and

apparently even a little dull, and who will roll
out plenty of good sound morality in a comfortable jog-trot way, with nothing to startle
or to excite, appeals very strongly to the representative citizen.   It reminds him of his minister (good man!) who, to be sure, puts him
regularly to sleep, but under whose ministra-
tions he feels that he can sleep with perfect
safety, knowing that no theological fences will
be broken down and no fine old dogmas shat-
tered.   This is precisely the reason why our
Presidents have nearly always been selected
because they were "safe" men rather than
political geniuses; and it may be that Mr.
Cleveland, who is by no means lacking in
shrewdness, has framed his oratorical style
with this very thought in mind.

There are, indeed, some indications that
did he but choose he might give utterance to
speeches in quite a different style.   Not many
of our Presidents have been known as makers
of epigrams or as fashioners of phrases; yet of
these few Mr. Cleveland ranks next to President Lincoln and President Grant.   Some of
the sentences and verbal combinations contained in his letters and messages are exceedingly crisp and pointed, and, in fact, they long
ago obtained a wide popular currency.   Such

is his famous maxim, "Public office is a public
trust," which Mr. Dana, of the *Sun*, declares
to be not original with Mr. Cleveland ; but as
nothing in this world is in reality original, this
criticism need not be taken very seriously.
Every one recalls the expressions "innocuous
desuetude," "offensive partisanship," "pernicious activity," and "ghoulish glee." Perhaps
we should also include "the communism of
pelf," a phrase exploited in his message to
Congress in 1888, though precisely what it
really means must remain uncertain. In some
of his State papers, also, while the form is still
Johnsonian, there may be found a point and
vivacity not visible in his formal speeches.
Several of his pension vetoes, in which he
exposed the absurdity of some malingering
claimant's case, were very neatly put. His
Venezuela message, too, was a bit of English
of which any one might be proud ; and one of
the London journals, even while condemning
the substance of it with great severity, felt
bound to speak of its language as marked by
"stateliness and force."

Finally, in several of his non-political speeches, when he perhaps felt less restraint in saying
what he had to say, there are passages which
abandon altogether the portentous and truistic

vein and exhibit quite unusual qualities.   Such
passages may be found in the speech that he
made at the Harvard celebration in 1886.   In
the intensely academic atmosphere of that interesting occasion, surrounded as he was by
scholars and men whose university associations
united them in a bond of intellectual brother-
hood, Mr. Cleveland spoke very simply and
naturally of his own regret that the circumstances of his life had given him no Alma
Mater; and in what he said there was a certain
suggestion of wistfulness, conveyed with great
dignity and good taste, that touched the hearts
of all who heard him.   On just one occasion
Mr. Cleveland has shown that he possesses a
fund of quaint humor and a gift for its expression.   This was in 1891, at a local celebration
near his former home on Cape Cod, when Mr.
Cleveland put aside his sesquipedalian manner
altogether and spoke just as a neighbor speaks
to neighbors, with perfect naturalness and ease,
and with many touches of quiet fun that one
may look for in vain in his other public utterances.   There was nothing the least forced about
it all, and it revealed a genial side to his character that was very winning.   Altogether, then,
one may rightly hold that Mr. Godkin's hypothesis (if indeed the hypothesis be Mr. God-

kin's) is very plausible ; and that Mr. Cleveland
may actually have adopted a labored and conventional style of oratory from a desire to win
confidence rather than applause, and to avoid
the snares that beset the possessor of a too
conspicuous cleverness.

If this was really his serious intention, he
was perhaps confirmed in it through the awful
example afforded by Mr. Chauncey M. Depew.
Mr. Depew, as every one knows, possesses a
rare union of sound judgment, vivid imagination, and lively wit, and is an adept in the art
of putting things to the multitude.   In the
early seventies it looked as though he intended
to cultivate this gift in a serious way and to
develop a style in which judgment and imagination should be the chief elements, with humor strictly subordinated to the other more
solid qualities.   Had he done so, there is no
doubt that he would have exercised a very
marked political influence. But either because
his defeat in New York State in 1872 put him
out of conceit with a purely political career,
or because the temptation to say good things
overpowered his discretion, he presently took
up the line of after-dinner speaking, with which
his name is now so generally associated.   His
after-dinner speeches are among the best of

their kind ; but to be known first of all as an
after-dinner speaker is to abandon any claim
upon serious consideration.   Once in a while
Mr. Depew will speak at length and with earnestness upon some weighty theme, and will
speak most admirably, but his hearers hardly
relish such an innovation, and persist in regarding him (we use the word in no offensive
sense) as a sort of public jester.   This means
the negation of any real influence; for no oratory can seriously sway the mind when each
person present, as he settles himself down
comfortably in his chair at the entrance of the
orator, displays upon his countenance the pre-
monitory flicker of an expectant grin.

Perhaps the best contemporaneous example
of self-restraint, and ease, and perfect taste in
public oratory is to be found in some of the
addresses of ex-President Harrison.   As a
speaker he is an instance of the curious development that seems to attend the occupancy
of the presidential office.   Before his election
he had for many years been in public life and
had spoken much ; yet no one ever regarded
him as having any especial facility as an orator.
In fact, while in the Senate he once made use
of the expression, " I lift up a prayer "—a form
of locution which suggests the stereotyped

vocabulary of the country prayer-meeting; and the *Post* of this city caught it up and rang the changes on it until the only thing that a mention of Mr. Harrison suggested to many intelligent citizens was the act of "lifting up a prayer." Nevertheless, as President, he never made a flat or feeble speech; but, on the contrary, surprised the whole country by the finish and ease of all his public utterances. Especially notable were the brief addresses that he made during his presidential progress across the continent, and above all to the audiences that met him in the Southern States. Here he was surrounded by those who were politically his opponents and against whom he, as a soldier, had fought in the days of the Civil War. It was no easy matter to speak a score of times under conditions such as these without saying anything to give offence, or else descending to the most *banal* conventionalities. Yet Mr. Harrison never once did either, but rose above all criticism in a series of little speeches that are perfect gems in their way—graceful, winning, suggestive, and tactful to a degree. In the longer addresses that he made during his tenure of the presidency, the same qualities are always present. One recalls especially his speech before the Peace Congress

at Washington, which was an oration marked
by equal dignity and urbanity, expressing as
it did a sympathetic approval of the aims of
his auditors while holding fast, as became the
guardian of the national honor, to the view
that, under existing conditions, the sword is
often the best auxiliary of the olive-branch.

Taking a retrospective glance at recent
American history, it is probable that of all the
speakers who have been heard in the national
forum during the past quarter of a century,
the most naturally gifted orator was General
Garfield. He had, indeed, many advantages
that other politicians have not often shared.
In the first place, he was one who, as Presidents go, must be regarded as a man of unusual cultivation. This attribute need not, indeed, be pressed too hard nor made too much
of, for it had its obvious limitations. He received, to be sure, while young, a college training; but it is not likely that anything more
than a glimmering of real culture could have
been imparted by Williams College as it was
some forty years ago, in spite of Mr. Garfield's
own much-quoted but rather absurd saying
about Mark Hopkins and the pine table. That
he subsequently exhibited attainments which
are rare among politicians is quite true; yet

now and then the limitations already mentioned would still appear and bear evidence
to the difficulty of escaping from early influences. Mr. Garfield had been at one time and
for a number of years a teacher, and in private
life something of the pedagogue kept always
cropping up in his fondness for advising his
friends as to what they ought to read, and in
his readiness to correct small errors of pro-
nunciation and of syntax.

This trait was curiously illustrated not long
before his death in an occurrence that, when
one considers the occasion, was almost grotesque. Soon after Guiteau had fired the
shot that was to prove so fatal, and while
General Garfield lay on his bed tormented
with ceaseless pain, a friend who had been
admitted to the room spoke a few words of
comfort.

" Mr. President," he said, " this thing has
blotted out all party feeling in the nation.
Every American to-day feels the deepest
sympathy for you."

The sufferer turned his face and spoke with
difficulty in a low, gasping voice:

"Sympathy *with*," said he, "not sympathy
for."

And later, when his death had been pro-

nounced inevitable, and some one asked him
to write a line with his name, as a last gift, he
traced these words:

Strangulatus pro republica.

Now, it was a little odd that at such a moment
he should have chosen to express himself in
Latin, and that, having chosen Latin, he
should employ this particular verb *strangu-
lare*, which, in the sense here given it, is perfectly classical and good, but somewhat rare.
It showed, indeed, his learning, but it showed
a certain pedantry as well.

Not always, however, did he have his erudition quite so well in hand. In the course of
his speech at the National Convention of 1880,
when he presented the name of Senator Sherman, he compared himself and his delegation
to Leonidas and the devoted band at Ther-
mopylæ, concluding with the words:

"And we shall stand firmly here, no matter
how many *Greeks* you may bring against us."

Which makes it clear that, for the moment
at least, his Greeks and his Persians were very
badly mixed.

At times, also, some slight evidences of defective taste were to be noticed by the careful
observer. We are inclined to describe as such

the scene when, after taking the inaugural oath upon the steps of the Capitol, he turned and kissed his mother, who was seated just behind him.   Of course, from one point of view, this thing was mighty fine, and it threw the editors of Sunday-school papers, both here and in England, into a prolonged ecstasy : yet we rather doubt whether in reality it was quite so fine after all ; for, apart from its being just the least bit too theatric, it most inappropriately injected the purely domestic relations of an individual into the midst of a supremely national ceremony, and one in which the stateliness and dignity of a great public function ought to have been the only thing before all minds.

However, with these few reservations, it may be unhesitatingly asserted that Mr. Garfield was, by nature and by training alike, a most impressive orator.   Next to Jefferson, and perhaps John Quincy Adams, he was of all our Presidents the most highly trained; and next to Mr. Arthur, who succeeded him, he was the most of a man of the world.   Wide reading, travel, and long intercourse with men of every type had given him a broad and comprehensive outlook ; and unlike most of our public men, he had thought out for himself the

views, both economic and political, that he
advocated; nor did he shuffle about in the
currents of changing opinion, as do those politicians who have no convictions of their own,
but wait subserviently upon the caprices of
the mob. He led rather than followed; and
this is why his speeches in Congress were not
mere ephemeral splurges, but are to this day
continual'y quoted for their apt and lucid
statement of fundamental truths. Unlike other party leaders, also, there was nothing petty
or personal in his treatment of political opponents. He struck hard blows, but they were
fair, and left no bitterness behind. As a man,
he made no enemies by his oratory; and he
gave the impression of a spirit too broad and
too nobly generous for petty altercations. Mr.
Garfield was singularly fortunate also in his
personal endowments. Gifted with a fine
presence, a resonant and expressive voice,
and an easy and singularly winning manner,
he charmed his listeners from the very first
sentences of an oration. He had, too, a certain sensuousness of temperament which with
a different environment and early training
might easily have developed into sensuality,
but which, in fact, merely imparted a richness
and warmth to his utterances, and indicated

only the virility which is absolutely essential to the successful orator, and which was so noticeable in Webster and in Clay. With all these qualities, then, both natural and acquired, Mr. Garfield stood forth, I think, as the very greatest of recent American orators ; and all his speeches, whether they be his carefully prepared deliverances in the halls of Congress or his spontaneous utterances upon the stump, are vivid, clean-cut, and forceful to a degree, marked everywhere by thought and imagination, with a certain large and luminous quality about them, and often rising into splendid and stirring eloquence.

Altogether, then, it is not easy to believe that the days of oratory have departed forever, that orators are born no more, and that men can never again be roused to action by the arts of eloquence ; but, as has been already stated, I believe that to-day it is only the occasion and theme that are momentarily lacking. Human nature does not change from generation to generation ; but its impulses and its elemental motives still remain the same. As it has always been true in the past, so will it always, I believe, be true throughout the future, that when great bodies of men are stirred by intense emotion and when the wind of passion is blowing over human hearts, then will the fire once more descend and touch the lips of some born orator, who will, as heretofore, smite down all opposition, take reason and imagination captive, and impose his single will on all who hear him, by the indescribable magic of the spoken word.

THE DOWNWARD DRIFT IN AMERICAN EDUCATION

THE DOWNWARD DRIFT IN AMERICAN EDUCATION*

FOR thirty years the development of American education has been almost wholly influenced by German teaching and example. Ever since the termination of the Civil War our students, in numbers that increase each year, have sought to supplement the training given them at home by spending one or more semesters at the German universities; the pædagogical ideas of German educators have been made accessible to every one through paraphrases and translations; the German methods have been universally accepted as the very best and soundest known; until at last we find the whole profession of American teachers leavened through and through by German thought.

This powerful and undisputed influence has been in many ways productive of a vast amount

* For permission to reprint this paper, acknowledgments are due to Mr. John Brisben Walker, of the *Cosmopolitan Magazine*, in which it originally appeared.

of good. In the first place, it has helped our
people to cut loose in all their intellectual life
and scholarly work from that ancient bondage
to English tradition which was received and
perpetuated throughout the long-protracted
period of American colonialism. For English
scholarship, as it existed a century or more
ago, when Gray and Gibbon styled the English universities " the home of bats and owls,"
was in many ways a thing of elegant sterility ;
and as handed down from generation to generation in our country, it wholly lost its ele-
gance and intensified its sterility. In the second place, the German influence taught the
practical and scientific value of thoroughness
—of all lessons the very hardest for Americans
to learn. The slipshod, happy-go-lucky optimism of our people, eager for quick results and
careless about perfection of form and accuracy
of detail, was nowhere, indeed, so unhappily
visible as in our scholarship. Isolated as
Americans long remained from all immediate
contact with an older and more finished civilization, they found it difficult to admit that
anything was better than their best ; and hence
mere show and superficial cleverness passed
current with the undiscriminating many, depriving them of any serious standards of com-

parison and cursing them with the fatuous self-complacency that is so fatal to all high achievement.

It was a revelation, then, to those stray pioneers of higher education who early in the sixties made their way to Heidelberg and Göttingen and Berlin to find at these great centres of learning what was to them a new and unknown intellectual life; to meet illustrious teachers who did not go over and over again with a monotonous *Nachbeterei* the rudimentary precepts of a text-book, but took for granted at the start the widest range of reading in their hearers; to watch investigators who set themselves the task of bringing to light what was unknown before, in laying bare the hidden, and augmenting by their work the sum of human knowledge; and to see gathered about these men a body of learners aflame with the noble enthusiasm of those whose ideal lies in the maximum and not in the minimum of achievement, and who fling themselves with all the passion of an intellectual crusade into the work of creative effort and discovery.

As a result of this new light upon methods of teaching and of learning, the old traditions of American education were swept away forever. The colleges and universities were nat-

urally the first to experience the change, and
then, as their students went out into the schools
and into the community at large, the whole
mass was leavened until, as I have said above,
our intellectual world was Germanized. A very
important adjunct of this change, and one that
made its swift accomplishment more easy, was
the enormous increase of the German element
in our population. In many of our larger
cities the proportion of citizens of German
birth is to-day actually in excess of the native-
born, and there are several States even where
the same preponderance prevails. It is therefore natural, as it is actually true, that the
German influence already noticed should not
only have been able to affect most radically
the American methods and theory of education, but that it should have extended to a
wider sphere and set its mark upon our social
and political philosophy. That in a single
generation a hitherto unknown interest in
German pædagogical doctrine should spring
up ; that the German language should dispute
with French its old-time place in the favor of
cultivated men and women ; and that German
literature should now be taught and read almost as widely as the more attractive literature
of France—these are but the superficial signs

of a very vital change. It is not too much to say that the influence of German thought, though directed first of all to a single phase of our development, has struck its roots down far more deeply; and that, aided by an ethnic change in our population, it has in reality effected a profound and somewhat startling alteration in the national character.

The American of a century ago was much more purely Anglo-Saxon than he is to-day. He still felt the dislike of all control, the impatience of restraint, and the strong individualism that had driven his ancestors from the England of Charles II., and that afterwards united them to defy the England of George III. Exulting in a sense of unrestricted freedom and an almost lawless largeness of vision, he felt himself equal to anything whatever. He had hewn out a home for himself with his own right arm, subduing the savage, the wild beast, and the illimitable forest; and he looked about him with something of the superb self-consciousness of a god, as he saw that his handiwork was very good. He was not a creature of rules and regulations; the most elemental principles of right and justice alone made up his simple code. He felt that character and energy together could accomplish anything, and he laughed to scorn the thought of dependence upon any one. And even later, in the early years of the present century, one notes the evidences of an extreme particularism. In political life we see prolonged the era of the small self-governing community, the era of the town-meeting, with a semi-patriarchal importance given to the family ; and in a wider field the sentiment of nationality still slumbering, a tenacious adherence to the doctrine of States' Rights, a distrust of centralization, and, in general, a firm belief in Jefferson's dictum, that "the best government of all is the one that governs least." So sturdily independent, so resentful even of favors, were Americans then that an English traveller records her astonishment on visiting the House of Representatives to see " member after member leaping to his feet to denounce with passionate indignation a bill which proposed to grant from the national treasury a sum of money for the development and extension of a system of public roads." The American feeling of that day was, in fact, most admirably typified in Daniel Boone, who needed nothing but his axe and rifle for his maintenance, and who felt that he was being stifled if he found another white man settling down within a hundred miles of him. It was an apotheosis of individuality, of self-reliance, and of personal power.

The German influence and the general alteration in the racial character of our people through incessant immigration have effectually changed all that; and to understand the change, one must consider for a moment what the mental attitude of the German really is. The typical German of the educated class is one who separates entirely his intellectual from his material life. He ascribes so much importance to the former, he has so much enthusiasm for its cult, that he views it as being in itself sufficient for the fulfilment of all his aspirations. Political conditions have for centuries intensified this tendency by excluding him from any really independent share in the larger public life, and thus forcing him back into his study or his lecture-room to think and theorize the more, because it is forbidden him to act. His life is, therefore, one of thought and not of action, and never is his thought conditioned by the various necessities that confront the man who tries to translate theory into terms of practice. Hence, it is always enough for the German if his notions be quite scientifically correct, if they be logical and lucid, if they be capable, in fact, of a sort of mathematical demonstration. He makes no allowance in his scheme for any difficulties that would attend its application by reason of the passions or the prejudices or the temperamental differences of actual men and women; for the personal equation has no place in his large and luminous philosophy, nor are the very unphilosophical facts of life permitted to disturb the symmetry of his hypothesis. That good old story of the German who was asked to write a paper about lions, and who had never seen or heard of lions, but who at once shut himself up in a darkened room until such time as he should have evolved the true conception of a lion from his inner consciousness, gives us in a humorous way a very faithful illustration of the German's mental attitude towards life. To him all problems whatsoever, whether social or political or philosophical, may be solved by taking thought; and the true solution is always capable of being summed up in a formula. If anything is wrong in life it is because the necessary formula for its amendment has not yet been properly worked out. If there are misery and sin and poverty and crime perceptible on every hand, all that is needed to banish them is a knowledge of the formula. If the State is nearly

shipwrecked by misgovernment or by the hostility of foreign powers, a simple formula will
set it right. Even character and morals and
temperament are reducible to formulaic treatment; and a true German, like Max Nordau,
will discover an incipient criminal in the greatest genius by simply getting at the measure-
ments of the base of his head, by examining
the tips of his ears, and by collecting the statistics of his similes and metaphors.

It is precisely here that American thought
to-day displays most strikingly the German influence. The cult of the formula has taken
root among us, and the extravagance of our
national devotion to it is proportionate to the
energy, and also to the childishness, of the
American people. The old-time American
knew nothing about formulas. He had no pre-
conceived and axiomatic theories about the
precise way in which things should be done.
He waited until the necessity came for doing
a particular thing, and then he just did it and
made no fuss about it. Take the drafting of
our national Constitution, for example. Of the
men who framed it, scarcely one was a political philosopher according to the German understanding of the term. They brought to
their task no carefully elaborated outfit of sci-

entific abstractions. They had simply studied
the political conditions that existed ; they understood the history and the temper of the
people; they grasped at once the practical
difficulties and the practical possibilities of the
problem, and they did their work accordingly.
Any able German thinker could, probably, in
half an hour point out a hundred absolutely
fatal defects in the Constitution which these
statesmen framed ; yet it has none the less en-
dured, with scarce a change, down to the present day, and the experience of every decade
only deepens the admiration with which men
view this splendid national charter, which has
served as a model for every republic founded
since that time.   On the other hand, the Germans had a chance in 1848 to show what
government by formula is like.   The political
philosophers swarmed in the Frankfort Assem-
bly of that year.   No one could doubt the
profundity of their learning ; they produced
some of the most beautiful formulas that even
Germany had been called on to admire ; yet
in just about six months the whole thing went
to smash, and ever since that day the German
people have cowered meekly down beneath the
booted heel of a military despotism such as a
typical Anglo-Saxon people would reduce to

pulp in the space of twenty-four good working hours.

But the modified American of to-day is as formula-ridden as any German ever was. He has worked out two general formulaic remedies for everything. In the sphere of politics and economics he has set up for himself the legislative formula as an infallible panacea ; while questions of every other sort he solves by the application of the educational formula. The legislative formula is supposed to be a substitute for the qualities that made the old-time American precisely what he was — for thrift and energy and self-reliance. The formula itself is an invocation of that mysterious and hazily defined Omnipotence which men impersonally call " the State," and which, in some inexplicable way, is supposed to have all power in heaven and earth to make men prosperous and happy, if only the appropriate formula can be devised in the shape of legislation. Thus we find in certain sections of the country the law invoked to make men temperate and sober ; in others, to make them chaste ; in still another, the Ten Commandments are to be enacted into statute law to make religion universal. If men, by reason of their own unthrift and reckless management, have lost their credit

22

at the banks, a law must instantly create new institutions for the special purpose of discounting all their paper. If, because of various economic conditions, the market prices of their products fall, a vote of Congress must at once reverse the universal laws of trade and screw up prices to a given figure. If money be scarce, the legislative formula will make it plenty, and assure to every man a comfortable balance at the bank. The American farmer of a century ago, if floods destroyed his crops or pestilence destroyed his cattle, just saved and worked and practiced self-denial till he had made good his losses. The American farmer of to-day does nothing of the kind. He simply lets his hair grow long and starts a new political party. In fact, though we call it in this country by another name, the spirit of American political theory to-day in every party is the helpless spirit of State Socialism — a purely German product, and one that has been spawned and nourished by the legislative formula.

The educational formula is equally in evidence among us. Just as the legislative formula is to make men prosperous and happy, so the educational formula is to make them wise and virtuous. Education can do anything, we are told, and every one is capable of

being educated, just as any one is capable of
being made an educator. It is a revival of
the old Socratic maxim that no one will vol-
untarily go wrong if he only knows the better
way. And in this the formulaic method is followed all along the line. There is first the educational formula itself, the alkahest, the universal solvent of our intellectual alchemists.
Then there is the formula for making the first
formula known, and the formula for inculcat-
ing the other formula; so that to-day we have
teachers who teach teachers to teach other
teachers how to teach. Everything is worked
out to the last degree of scientific exactness.
The individual idiosyncrasy of the learner does
not count. There is a psychological formula
which reduces all intellects and all capacities
to a common denominator, and everything can
now be done by a set of scientific rules, from
the time required per diem for teaching each
division and subdivision of a topic to the precise manner in which that topic must be taught,
almost down to the cut of the teacher's clothes.
Formerly it was believed that there must be a
certain adaptability in the instructor, a certain
regard for the needs of the individual learner;
but that has been done away with now. In
these days the scientific educator in the pri-

mary schools draws spidery little diagrams, in which a crooked line goes wriggling up a sort of trellis; and this psychological horoscope, all carefully marked out in accordance with a set of definite rules, saves every one a world of trouble in deciding on his methods. Education nowadays, in fact, is being desiccated and formulated and reduced to the compact and convenient shape of a set of logarithmic tables. All this, of course, is here quite strongly put. In detail and in particular instances it is subject to qualifications and exceptions; but as a characterization of existing tendencies it is absolutely true.

A natural corollary of such a state of doctrine is the popular assumption that anything whatever can be taught. Hence comes a proposition which is logically sound enough and theoretically unobjectionable: that in the rapidly expanding curricula of our colleges and universities those subjects of instruction should appear which bear directly on the personal welfare of the student in his future life, and that his moral and social, as well as his intellectual, needs should be provided for. If we teach him languages and literatures and philosophy and history to make him an accomplished gentleman, and if we teach him chemistry and mechanical engineering to enable him to earn an income, why not also teach him those things that are vastly more important for his real happiness? Why should not the young and inexperienced undergraduate in the formative period of his early life learn from the lips of university instructors everything that makes for a rational, virtuous, and successful life— how to preserve his health, how to resist temptation, how to choose his profession, how to avoid mistakes in business, how to invest his money, how to select a wife, how to bring up children, and how to grow old gracefully? These things are really most important—they are even vital; and why should not the universities make the teaching of them a matter of most serious concern? Why not, indeed? The thought is very beautiful and pleasing. In fact, if all the blessings of the legislative formula shall finally be added to the equally beneficent effects of the educational formula, what a glorious world this world of ours will be! When legislation finally assures to every citizen a princely income, and makes him chaste and temperate and earnestly religious, and when education gives him perfect wisdom, unbroken health, a thoroughly congenial occupation, exemption from all business troubles, a fascinating wife, and children that shall fill his heart with pride, then truly we shall all be living, not merely in Utopia, but in Paradise.

The great defect in all this sort of argument, so far as it relates to education, is precisely that which vitiates so many of the German theories. It takes no notice whatsoever of the facts of man's experience, and it is based upon the fallacy that all possible subjects of teaching stand upon precisely the same basis. It does not carefully distinguish, as one is ultimately forced to do, between the facts of which a purely intellectual knowledge is sufficient to afford a reasonable grasp and those other facts to which this knowledge can of itself give no real practical importance. For instance, by drilling any man of average intelligence in the necessary rules and principles, it is entirely possible to make of him a tolerable mathematician, because when once he knows those rules and principles he has done what is essential. In like manner you can, by your mere teaching, make a sort of linguist of him, or a grammarian, or a bibliographer; but you cannot, on the other hand, by any possible amount of formal precept or instruction or exhortation, endue him with sobriety or continence or prudence or practical wisdom. And why? Sim-

ply because in all these things mere knowledge
is not half enough ; but it may be, as it usually
is, a thing entirely apart from practice. The
knowledge that merely knows is a very different thing from the conviction that dominates
and deters. One may to some extent be drawn
from teaching, but the other can come from
grim experience alone. Is it, indeed, through
lack of knowledge that most men violate the
laws of life? Are those who drink themselves
to death not perfectly aware of what they are
about? Are the gluttons and the dissolute
supremely ignorant of what will ultimately
happen to them? Does not one hear men
every day declare that such and such a thing
is killing them, but that they cannot bring
themselves to give it up? And are not these
things oftenest found among the very class
that is made up of educated men and women?

> "Video meliora proboque,
> Deteriora sequor "

is a confession that is at once both older and
more modern than the time of Ovid, who first
wrote it down. It might, indeed, quite truth-
fully be made by every one who has fully and
freely lived the life of the larger world. All
human history is rich in illustrations of how

wide the gulf is which divides mere knowledge from the will and purpose to apply it: Seneca heaping up a colossal fortune and sitting down before a table wrought of beaten gold to write a philosophic tract on the curse of avarice and the blessings of simplicity and poverty; Thomson, who never left his pillow before noon, lying in bed and composing enthusiastic lines on the delights of early rising; and quite recently, that blend of saint and satyr, Paul Verlaine, reeling home from a long debauch in the foulest stews of Paris to set down with trembling hand an outburst filled with passionate adoration of the God of Purity. If only teaching could make human beings wise and good, the world would long ago have welcomed the millennium, for surely there has been no lack of teaching since the time when men first came to see the link that binds effect to cause. Through all the centuries the moralist has moralized, the philosopher has explained, the father has exhorted and advised, the mother has pleaded; and the young have listened to it all, and then gone on their own way unconvinced. And through the centuries, also, the priests have taught, calling to their aid the arts of eloquence and the promises and threatenings of religion, appealing to every motive

that can sway the mind—now promising in
words as sweet as honey the splendors of
immortal life and endless happiness, and now
blasting the imagination with fearful pictures
lighted by the glaring fires of hell. Does any
one suppose that what duty and affection and
pity and hope and terror, backed up by strenuous eloquence and religious faith, have never
yet accomplished, can be effected by the kindly talk of a sleek university professor in some
intercalated college course? What possible
impression could be made in this way by even
the very wisest and shrewdest and most eminent of teachers? A group of young men with
the hot blood of youth running riot in their
veins, their hearts on fire with passion and
stung by an œstrus-like desire to fathom for
themselves the secrets of the unknown life
that lies in all its strange, mysterious fascination just beyond the college walls—how much
will the teaching of another man's experience
stand for in the minds of such as these? Some
mewling milksop here and there may possibly
accept that teaching and remember it ; but
mewling milksops do not count in the general
scheme of life. And as to some of these proposed additions to the university curriculum,
the humor of the proposition strikes one rather

forcibly. When a young man is about to fall
in love, can any one imagine him referring
gravely to his note-books to see whether the
conditions are exactly suitable, and whether
the professorial formula applies? And one
would like to ask whether it is contemplated
to give a practical and convincing turn to the
instruction, as is necessary even in far less important subjects. Is the university to offer
several electives in experimental courtship,
and is there to be established a laboratory of
love?

No; it is just as true to-day as it was true
five thousand years ago, and as it will be true
five thousand years from now, that the most
vital and important facts of life cannot be
taught by academic training, but must be
learned by every human being for himself. It
is a hard saying; but it expresses nothing but
the fact of human limitation—the limitation
that serves as a line beyond which mankind
can never go; for if the experience of the past
could be accumulated, and if the youth of to-
day could be at once equipped with all the
garnered wisdom of his ancestors, and if every
generation could add to this its own experience intact, the race of men would cease to
be mere mortals, but would rise above the

level of humanity and be as the immortal
gods.

The fact is, that so far from adding to the
subjects now included in the university curriculum, we should, instead, diminish them.
The present craze for making that curriculum
a common dumping-ground for every possible
variety of instruction is the most unfortunate
of all the tendencies that are visible in educational theory to-day. As we have imitated
the Germans in so many things, it is a lasting
pity that we have not seen fit to imitate them
also in excluding the teaching of the purely
mechanical arts from university instruction and
in shutting them off into the polytechnicum,
where they properly belong. When machine-
shops and factories and all the paraphernalia
of the applied sciences are imported into the
academic shades, and when the perfume of
the Attic violet is stifled by the stenches of
the chemist's crucible, the true purpose of the
university is forgotten, and its higher mission is in a great measure sacrificed; for
then there can exist no longer a distinct and
definite type of university-man. The civic
value of the university in times now past
was this: it gave to the community a very
special class, not only highly trained, and

trained in a broad and liberal way, but trained
also according to one particular standard and
with an absolute identity of training. This
identity of training bound all university-men
together by the strongest possible ties of sympathy and mutual understanding, so that they
stood forth as a sort of Sacred Band, alike in
private and in public life, exercising an influence for serenity and sanity of thought whose
value was inestimable and out of all proportion
to the actual numbers of the ones who exercised it. From this class came the men who
laid so firmly the foundations of the American
Republic, and who worked out in a broad, far-
seeing way the basal principles of our constitutional law and public polity; for of this class
were Hamilton and Jefferson and Jay and Madison and Webster and Calhoun and Adams.
They all received the older college training,
based not upon the bread-and-butter principle, but upon the nobler and far loftier conception of what the highest education means.
But at the present time the curious belief that
all subjects of study are in themselves equally important is dragging into the sphere of
university teaching anything and everything
which the casual person may desire to know;
and worse than this, it is putting upon every

DOWNWARD DRIFT IN AMERICAN EDUCATION 349

grade of capacity and attainment the self-same stamp of approval. Yet those who argue for this equality of value in the subjects taught do not regard the products of such teaching as being equal. They do not rank a great fly-paper manufacturer with a great statesman, nor a great cheese-monger with a great lawyer or physician. But when we hear to-day that So-and-so is a university-man, one never knows by reason of that fact alone whether this person is in reality a gentleman and a scholar, or whether he is only a sublimated type of tinker. And now that this confusion has been thoroughly established, what intimate and universal bond of sympathy can possibly exist among the scions of a university? The university has, in fact, been swamped by the influx of the mob, and its inmates are themselves becoming only an unconsidered fraction of that mob. In other words, the so-called "liberal" policy in university government has not raised mediocrity to the plane of scholarship, but has degraded scholarship to the plane of mediocrity. It has been in every sense a process of levelling down; in no sense has it been a process of levelling up. This, then, is gradually blotting out the true value of the university as a factor in the nation's larger life.

By throwing its doors wide open to every one and for every purpose, and by losing all perception of its original design, its chief importance and its noblest influence are vanishing away—lost in the wellnigh universal reign of the commonplace.

Linked closely with many other very serious educational mistakes, and from many points of view by far the most profoundly serious of them all, is that curious fancy, which is almost universal among our people, that education in itself and for all human beings is a good and thoroughly desirable possession. So axiomatic is this held to be that its principle has been incorporated into the constitutions of many of our States, and not only is education made free to all, but in most States it is made compulsory upon all. There is probably in our whole system to-day no principle so fundamentally untrue as this, and there is certainly none that is fraught with so much social and political peril for the future. For education means ambition, and ambition means discontent. Now, discontent is in itself a divine thing. When it springs up in a strong creative intellect capable of translating it into actual achievement, it is the mother of all progress; but when it germinates in a limited and feeble

brain it is the mother of unhappiness alone.
Yet the State decrees that all shall have some
share of education—that is, some share of discontent; and as the vast majority of minds
are limited and feeble, compulsory education
means everywhere compulsory discontent.
Could anything be more fatuous or more
dangerous from a statesman's point of view?
The thoroughly pernicious fruits of such a
policy are already visible. We see on every
hand great masses of men stirred by a vague
dissatisfaction with their lot, their brains
addled and confused by doctrine that is only
half the truth and vaguely understood, yet
thoroughly adapted to make them ripe for
the work of the agitator and the enemy of
public order. We see the farms deserted by
young men who flock to the already crowd-
ed cities in the hope of ease and fortune,
and by young women whose attainments fit
them to be admirable dairy-maids, but who
aspire to be artists and musicians. Such education as these possess can never qualify for
any serious *rôle;* it only makes for grievous
disappointment and a final heart-break. Nor
is there any moral safeguard in a limited degree of education. Quite the contrary. It
only makes the naturally criminal person far

more dangerous, converting the potential sneak-thief into the actual forger and embezzler and the bar-room brawler into the anarchistic bomb-thrower. Statistics lately sent to Congress in a veto message show the fact that in our prisons the proportion of the fairly educated to the uneducated is far larger than among an equal number of ordinary citizens. And this is due to the ill-considered system which forces a half-education on all men, whether they will or no, thus breeding for the State some of its most difficult sociological problems. A sounder policy would make the way to education easy, but not free to all. In minds that nature has adapted for development discontent will spontaneously arise, and these minds will of their own accord strive upward. Let these find education easy of attainment, since they are fitted for it; but more than this no philosophical legislator to-day should advocate or desire.

The summing up of the whole matter, then, is this: the outlook of our educational future is very far from bright. A mistaken notion of the use and value of education now prevails, which, in a sphere of elementary teaching, is preparing danger for society and for the State by looking far too strictly at mere theory and by ignoring fact; while in the sphere of university training the only safeguard against these growing evils is being gradually swept away. To seek to stem the tide of tendency is to-day an idle task, and one can only wait and hope for a reaction and a very radical reversion to the sounder practice of the past. With the modern scientific modes of teaching, and with an apparatus far beyond what other centuries ever knew, the philosophic thinker can imagine a university ideal which may some day perhaps be brought to pass. But the key to it all is the true conception of what higher education really means. The university does not exist to train mere sordid toilers and to help them to make money. We do not need more baccalaureate bagmen, more "hustlers," more matriculated mechanics, more polymathic plumbers. We have too many of them now. Its purpose should be something higher—to teach serenity of mind and loftiness of purpose, to make men see straight and think clearly, to endue them with a sense of proportion and a luminous philosophy of life—a thing impossible to those who do not draw their inspiration from the thought, the history, and the beauty of the classic past. It should produce for the service of the State men such as those who in

23

the past made empires and created common-
wealths—a small and highly-trained patriciate,
a caste, an aristocracy, if you will. For every
really great thing that has been accomplished
in the history of man has been accomplished
by an aristocracy. It may have called itself a
sacerdotal aristocracy, or a military aristocracy,
or an aristocracy based on birth and blood ;
yet these distinctions were but superficial, for
in reality it always meant one thing alone—the
community of interest and effort in those whose
intellectual force and innate gift of government
enabled them to dominate and control the destinies of States, driving in harness the hewers
of wood and drawers of water, who constitute
the vast majority of the human race, and whose
happiness is greater and whose welfare is more
thoroughly conserved when governed than
when trying to govern. From the small, compact, and efficient body of free citizens who,
amid the unfree and disfranchised, made up
the aristocracies of Athens and of Sparta, and
the patrician class in Rome down to the gentlemen of England, this has been always true,
and not because of the ostensible reason of
their domination, but because they gathered
to themselves and made their own all that was
best and strongest in the nation, opening the

way for genius wherever it was found and working out those great results that stand as monuments of human power. A caste, an aristocracy of intellect like this, might still be bred in our American universities would they but thrust out of their precincts the faddists and the utilitarians, exclude the factories and workshops and all the polytechnic patchwork that make of the university curriculum to-day a thing of rags and tatters, and retain only the humanities and the liberal arts. Then they might once more give to the service of the nation men of high breeding and supreme attainments, who would rise above the level of the commonplace to establish justice and maintain truth, to do great things in a large and splendid way, and to illustrate and to vindicate the majesty of man.

QUOD MINIME RERIS

QUOD MINIME RERIS

THERE is something partly pathetic and partly exasperating in the reflection that the vast majority of mankind, on nearly every important subject, get their facts and their opinions wholly at second hand. Close to the heart of each great problem, whether it be theological or political or scientific or philosophical, a few powerful and unwearied minds are always laboring and watching, forgetful of self, single-minded, devoted to one sublime ideal—the discovery of truth, cost what it may and point whither it will. They have no thought of gain, no love of popular applause, no motive save the scholar's motive, which is, at its highest, so pure and so disinterested as almost to deserve the name of sacred. Whatever knowledge men have gleaned as yet in each respective field is known to them, and they live in serene contentment, and die with a smile of happiness, if they can but feel that by their labor and self-denial the sum of hu-

man knowledge has been perceptibly aug-
mented, that through their effort a single ray
of light has stolen out a little further into the
dusk of the Unknown.   They seek absolutely
nothing for themselves, and what they learn
is free to all who care to take it from them.

There stands about these men a second
class—shrewd, clever, quick·witted, and ingenious, having much of the scholar's knowledge and very little of the scholar's spirit,
with eyes that are turned towards the world at
large, which is, in fact, their oyster.   Whatever
stream of knowledge flows forth from the little
sanctuary where the giants of learning smite
the rocks of difficulty, these brilliant persons
rapidly scoop it up into their own shallow vessels, and diluting it with the water of the first
roadside puddle, run abroad throughout the
world, selling the draught to any one who may
seek to buy.   To drop the figure, it is, in general, only the adapter, the popularizer, the
actual dispenser, whom the world at large en-
counters ; and it is, therefore, to him that the
glory and the praise of the discovery are given.
Take almost any field of science, using that
term in its broadest sense, and ask the average
man to tell you the great contemporary names
suggested by it, and he will always give you

the names of middlemen, of men who sit in
the outer gates of learning and not within the
penetralia. Hence it is (to take two obvious
illustrations) that the multitude regard Mr.
Edison as a great master of electrical experiment, and view Professor Max Müller as chief
among comparative philologists.

It is in the sphere of religious and theological discussion that this curious and rather de-
pressing phenomenon is most strikingly perceptible, because such topics have from time
immemorial most vitally and continuously interested the greatest number of human beings. And here the story is the same. A few
profoundly learned men, equipped with all the
means of investigation known to this last and
greatest of the centuries, are laboring in the
difficult field of Biblical research, animated by
no controversial ardor, heedless of fame, and
seeking only in a reverent spirit to eliminate
error and to know the entire truth as God has
given men to see it. Theirs is the knowledge
of text and times, of the subtlest linguistic
coloring, of the nicest questions of evidence, of
the testimony that comes from within, and of
the corroboration or contradiction that exists
in the perplexing records of external history.
They work on, and under their hands the light

appears to grow less dim. Of the problems
before them, some seem to contain the possibility of a plain solution ; there is something
at least that can be clearly learned. But they
know that the last word has not yet been
spoken, and that they have lifted only a little
corner of the veil. The time has not arrived
for any man to speak with full authority ; and
they still work on. But all about them are
flitting other and restless minds eager for something new, impatient of delay, filled with the
spirit of the intellectual charlatan and the sen-
sation-monger ; and these men snatch greedily
at the scraps that fall from the sober table of
the wise, and rush off to proclaim a new doctrine and to dedicate some structure hastily
reared upon a foundation that will not for one
moment bear a serious strain. They write
books and magazine articles, and even letters
in the newspapers ; and they bask complacent-
ly in the sunshine of popular amazement.

Upon these there waits still another class—
the shallow, superficial, fluent preachers who
combine the *flair* of a trained reporter with
the ambitions of a popular actor. They
are filled with the modern notion that the
teaching of religion — the most solemn and
impressively awful responsibility that can rest

upon a human being—is of value only in so
far as it can be made amusing or exciting or
picturesque. These are the men who put off
the external marks of their calling, who dress
like commercial travellers, who slap you on
the back, assume an air of brisk joviality,
preach bicycle sermons, organize sports and
pastimes for their flock, and conceive the
idea of " church smokers " as a means of grace.
This sort of thing they speak of in their own
jargon as " meeting men as men," " bringing
religion down from the clouds," and " making
it practical "; not seeing that their unseemly
and grotesque impersonation is viewed by
men of the world with something of that half-
amused, half-pitying contempt with which one
would behold a middle - aged school - mistress
capering in a skirt-dance. The eternal themes
of reverence and mercy, of justice and of judgment, are wholly absent from their clack, and
they can tell you far more about duck-shooting
and the gossip of the clubs.

When, then, the middlemen of doctrine, the
theological jerry-builders, send out some new
report of what they say has been discovered
by serious and scientific scholars, this half-
explained and half-digested bit of knowledge
is snapped up in a flash. It is, very likely,

only part of a preliminary study, a tentative
hypothesis, a theory broached as being one of
several possible explanations; or it may represent only one stage of an investigation which
is still in progress and of which the final results
may wholly alter the actual significance of the
earlier assumption. But all this makes no difference to the clerical seeker after a sensation.
He hastily reads an article or two in the magazines, runs over a popular book upon the subject, gets a general notion of what it is all
about, hits upon a few catchwords and effective phrases, and then feels himself fully prepared to discuss the whole history of Biblical
criticism from Thomas of Heraclea to Tischen-
dorf and Gregory. This leads men, especially newspaper-men, to describe him as "fully
abreast of the times," or perhaps even as "an
up-to-date divine." If the particular information that has filtered its way down to him is,
on the face of it, a little subversive of pre-
viously accepted notions, something with a
flavor of heterodoxy about it, he is especially
well pleased. Nothing delights a clergyman
of this type more than to utter radical senti-
ments and views that to many are perhaps a
little shocking—especially when put, as he too
often puts them, with a half-humorous treat-

ment of a sacred theme, or a jocular version of
some Biblical narrative. He knows that there
is something peculiarly piquant in heterodoxy
when it is preached from an orthodox pulpit,
though the same utterances would fall absolutely flat and unnoticed if proclaimed by one
without the pale. Therefore he smugly keeps
a tight hold upon the temporalities of his
charge while playing all the time with heresy;
and if he can only get some one to accuse him
of being an actual heretic, his future is assured;
for then the newspapers will print abstracts of
his sermons, and he will be known both far and
wide as a " liberal " and " modern " man.

Not all who set forth in their sermons what
they think to be the truth established by the
higher criticism are men of this cheap type.
There are scores of conscientious teachers,
who themselves are troubled by the assaults
upon tradition, and who vaguely feel the spiritual danger that lurks in much that is put forth
by those who claim to know the latest doctrine
of the critics. Yet these men, from the very fact
of their conscientiousness, hold that it would
be quite dishonest to conceal the facts as they
have come to understand them. So they load
up their discourses with questions of textual
and exegetical subtlety; speaking of the doubt-

ful authorship of one or another of the sacred
writings, of the chronological uncertainty of a
record long regarded as inspired, of pseudonymous epistles, of the early canon, of interpolations, and incorporated glosses. They do not
see that the fundamental truths of Christian
doctrine, its ethics and its true divinity, are
not in the least affected by things like these.
They forget that the obligation and the moral
beauty of charity and chastity are not dependent upon one view or another of a chronological date; that the Aramaic coloring of a proph-
et's style cannot impair the eternal validity of
justice; that the double authorship of a Biblical record does not lessen the inherent sanctity
of an honest, reverent, and blameless life; that
the peculiar significance of a particle askew has
no bearing upon the need which all men feel of
hope and consolation in their hours of sorrow.
And, again, they do not see how, nevertheless,
these paltry scraps of third-hand scepticism,
when imparted to the multitude, do actually
undermine and honeycomb the foundation of
a faith upon which must ultimately rest those
motives that alone lead men to strive for a better and a purer and a nobler life. What does
the layman gather from a homily replete with
all the jargon of a transcendental critic? Noth-

ing whatever beyond a vague impression that
all the teaching learned by him at his mother's
knee—the teaching that has kept alive within
him all the better aspirations of his nature—
is doubtful, obsolete, or even false. And then
as time goes on he comes to think that right
and wrong are nothing but conventionalities
when all is so uncertain, that life's philosophy
is only hedonism, that there is no changeless
standard of morality, and that an enlightened
selfishness is in reality the highest wisdom.
It *may* be otherwise, he will tell you, but he
doesn't know; and when religious teachers are
themselves in doubt, why should he acknowl-
edge any personal responsibility? Thus the
process of disintegration spreads, and thus the
teachers of religion are themselves unconsciously converted into mere assistant infidels.
And all the while, above and beyond these
untrained babblers of a doctrine still chaotic
and half-understood, the dispassionate, untir-
ing students who are seated at the sources go
on and on and on, discarding one by one their
own first tentative hypotheses, proving the
falsity of their own first radical assumptions,
and quickly leaving far behind them their own
crude generalizations, even while the superficial pulpit orator is still endeavoring to master

these and to promulgate them as being the ultimate and supreme expression of discovered truth.

A truly monumental work by Professor Adolf Harnack, of which the first part not long ago appeared, suggests inevitably the train of thought that has been here outlined. Professor Harnack is himself unquestionably viewed by Biblical scholars as being the most eminent of all the students who are to-day investigating the history and the sources of early Christian literature. As a chronologist he has no superior, and he is deeply read in all the existing records of the period that is his chosen field of scientific investigation. His elaborate *Dogmengeschichte*, only lately translated into English, has been, since its first appearance in 1889, a standard work with investigators of every school of thought. He is not an orthodox theologian; in fact, his name has in the past been many a time invoked for the discomfiture of the adherents of orthodox tradition. But he is a type of the scholar who is absolutely free from any trace of intellectual vanity, and his frankness and generosity and candor have won for him the respect and even the admiration of those who have most earnestly opposed his critical judgments. He is one of those rare spirits who feel it to be no shame, but rather a most honorable duty, to retract beliefs which further light has shown to be erroneous, and who with a single heart desire to establish nothing but the truth.

The work referred to just above as having recently appeared contains a most minute and searching exposition of a part of his investigations in the chronology of the first two centuries of the Christian era, and to these he has prefixed an Introduction written in a singularly luminous and forceful style, and summarizing the general conclusions to which his long and patient toil has led him. This lucid statement of the attitude of perhaps the greatest living scholar towards some of the most vexatious problems of New Testament criticism must necessarily arouse a very general interest ; and it may be very specially commended to the notice of those dabblers in theology whose minds still feel the influence of Baur and Strauss, and who regard a tincture of the Tübingen teaching as the mark of erudite and enlightened liberalism.

For the benefit of the general reader, it may be useful to recall briefly the attitude assumed by those investigators who, with perfect honesty but with imperfect data, laid the foun-

24

dations of the particular school which so
grievously unsettled the minds of all who
let themselves be dazzled by its learning
and impressed by its audacity. Of these
destructive critics, Ferdinand Christian Baur,
"the Niebuhr of New Testament criticism,"
and one imbued with the Hegelian view of
history, professed to see in the books of the
New Testament evidence of a period of storm
and stress in the early days, of a period when
discordant passion rent the Church asunder
and filled with bitterness and resentment the
factions that contended over questions of ec-
clesiastic polity.   Closely following Baur came
Strauss, as ingenious, brilliant, and profound
as he, and more aggressively radical than De
Wette, his other predecessor, whose methods,
in fact, as applied by him to the study of the
Old Testament, Strauss now directed upon the
New.   Under his dissolving touch the Gospels
seemed to melt into mist and myth; miracle,
prophecy, faith itself, appeared to shrink to
nothingness.   His keen analysis seemed based
upon irrefutable fact, and the charm of his
style carried his teaching to minds that seldom note the varying phases of theological
discussion.   The influence of his *Leben Jesu*
it would be difficult to overrate.   Upon timor-

ous souls of the Robert Elsmere type the effect
was overwhelming, while others who shrank
from the bold logic of Strauss still received
something of his scepticism through less po-
lemical works, among which perhaps Renan's
Histoire des Origines may be regarded as most
influential. Probably not many English and
American theologians went all the length that
Strauss would logically lead them; but there
is not a doubt that much which he professed
to demonstrate found lodgment in the minds
of many men, especially in those of teachers
of religion. Many perhaps did not at once
confess to being influenced by what they read;
but it is certain that their former faith, their
feeling of certainty, yielded gradually to the
solvent of this German revelation, and that in
time their attitude became and has remained
the attitude of men who doubt. As Professor
Harnack himself declares:

"There was a time—in fact, the general public has
not gone beyond it yet — when the oldest Christian
literature, including the New Testament itself, was
looked upon as but a tissue of deceptions and falsifi-
cations. . . . There is still left . . . an undefined
sense of distrust, a method like that of a suspicious
government which is always fastening itself on single
points, and which attempts by means of them to at-

tack conclusions that are clear and definite. . . . An
effort is now made to trace all sorts of 'tendencies,'
and to point out extensive interpolations; or else a
scepticism is visible which places probability and im-
probability on precisely the same level."

Now it is to be presumed that both the
Tendenzkritik and the scepticism of which
Professor Harnack is here speaking are far
less universal in this country than in Germany; yet they certainly exist, and they exist,
too, in minds in which their presence is not
generally suspected. But their existence undoubtedly depends upon a strong feeling that
they are in accordance with the matured and
well-established opinions of the very ablest
scholars. Our doubting Thomases, in fact,
have not yet got beyond the era of Baur and
Strauss; and they imagine that the views of
Baur and Strauss are still substantially the
views that German critics hold to-day. They
know, of course, that the work of investigation
is still going on; but they are absolutely un-
aware that its trend is by no means the same
as that which characterized the scholarship of
the early sixties. Hence, it is extremely interesting, and to the majority even of Biblical
students it must be almost startling, to come
upon a frank, dispassionate statement of re-

sults like those set forth in Professor Harnack's Introduction. To feel their full significance and weight, it should again be noted
that this writer is everywhere acclaimed as
being the very ablest and most conscientious of
those scholars who approach the subject from
the side of purely secular and scientific criticism.

What, then, is the deliberate judgment of
this eminent investigator with regard to the
questions that have just been mentioned?
Coming to his task with a thorough disbelief
in the accuracy of the Christian traditions, and
standing even to-day without the pale of or-
thodoxy, Professor Harnack states, nevertheless, that the conclusions which he has reached
are in all important points in harmony with
these same traditions. The irresistible logic
of chronology, the marshalling of an infinite
array of significant facts, have led him with
most admirable candor to set down this very
remarkable confession :

"The oldest literature of the Church in all important points and in most of its details is, from the point
of view of literary criticism, both genuine and worthy
of reliance. In the whole New Testament there is in
all probability only a single writing [the Second Epis-
tle of Peter] that can be looked upon as pseudonymous
in the strict sense of the word."

He then goes on to say that, even of the uncanonical writings, those that are pseudony- mous are surprisingly few; that in the case of one at least (the so-called *Acta Theclæ*) its pseudonymity was recognized and condemned by the Church itself; that there are few writ- ings that are interpolated, and that the inter- polations themselves are mainly harmless.

"The literary tradition of the Pre-Catholic Period is shown to be, as a whole, reliable."

But these general statements, striking though they be, do not exhaust the list of Professor Harnack's remarkable admissions. Practically he accepts all of the Pauline Epistles as genuine, though the dates which he defends differ by a few years from those of the Church tradition. He gives a chronology of St. Paul's life, which removes the last doubt, based on external evi- dence, against the authenticity of these writ- ings. He points out the internal evidence which each of the Gospels affords as testimony to the genuineness of the others. He states without qualification that the letters of Igna- tius and of Polycarp are all authentic, and he admits with a generous frankness the inaccuracy of the view upon this subject which he himself would have defended ten years ago. Most im-

pressive of all is his broad and immensely significant summing up, in which he boldly asserts
that the whole drift of critical thought to-
day is not destructive, but conservative (he
calls it "reactionary"), and that he looks for a
strengthening of this tendency in the immediate future.

"The chronological succession in which tradition
has placed the original documents of Christianity is,
in all essential points, from the Epistles of Paul to the
writings of Irenæus, correct; and it forces the historian to disregard all theories whatever relating to
these events, if they conflict with this succession."

It is eminently desirable that these conclusions of so learned and dispassionate a scholar
may soon be very widely known. They surely
will correct the false assumption that a sneak-
ing scepticism in religious teaching is in any
sense a proof of erudition or of liberality of
thought; and they may possibly bring back
to a more sober way of thinking those whose
convictions have been unsettled by a mistaken
adherence to mere critical authority. Then
we may see, perhaps, far fewer "up-to-date
divines" and more of those simple-mannered
priests who do not study fashion in their faith
and change it with each season of the year;

but who live quietly among their flocks, shar-
ing their sorrows and their joys, and teaching
them, not the latest thing in dittography and
haplography, but instead those homely virtues
that can never age, and that in every century
bind men together and make for unity and
purity and untroubled peace.

Yet vastly more important than the actual
conclusions to which Professor Harnack has
attained is the evidence which this volume
gives us of how shifting and uncertain at the
best is purely secular learning. What this
great critic held as truth ten years ago he now
repudiates as falsehood ; what his predecessors
stated with dogmatic certainty, even the most
radical of modern Biblical investigators have
long ago rejected. It is an impressive lesson
to every one who is tempted to yield up some
portion of historic faith to the winds of secular
authority, to be blown about with every fitful
gust ; for, looking back over long periods of
years, critics recant, their teaching perishes ;
and that which stands immutable and quite
secure is the great tradition and the mighty
system that perpetuate whatever is best and
highest in human aspiration and belief. Mere
scholarship grows obsolete and is discredited ;
but the pages over which the scholar pores

still lend to the troubled soul the consolation of inspired wisdom, while the splendid structure that has been reared upon their teaching is the one and only thing that, amid the wreck of theory, the mist of casuistry, and the supreme assault of intellectual pride, has never for a single moment yet been shaken.

THE END

www.ingramcontent.com/pod-product-compliance
Lightning Source LLC
Chambersburg PA
CBHW030904270326
41929CB00008B/570